Build Your Own BASIC

From Scratch

Richard (Dick) Whipple

D1662736

Build Your Own BASIC – From Scratch

Richard (Dick) Whipple
Visit my website at www.whippleway.com

Printed in the United States of America

First Printing: January 2020
Amazon Kindle (Paperback)

ISBN 9781659041095

Table of Contents

Preface _____ 7

Chapter 1 Computer Programs _____ 8

Computer Languages_____ 8

Language Design _____ 11

    Flow _____ 11

    Structure _____ 12

    Modularity_____ 13

*Chapter 2 The BYOC-24 CPU*_____ 16

BYOC-24 CPU Specification _____ 16

BYOC-24 Instruction Set _____ 17

    1. Register Operations _____ 18

    2. Data RAM and ROM Access _____ 19

    3. Index Register Operations _____ 20

    4. Arithmetic/Logic Operations _____ 20

    5. Miscellaneous Operations _____ 21

    6. Subroutines _____ 23

    7. Jumping and Branching_____ 25

*Chapter 3 Assembly Language*_____ 27

Subroutine Libraries _____ 27

High/Low Guessing Game Library_____ 30

The "Setup" Code Segment_____ 31

The "Main Loop" Segment _____ 32

Testing an Assembly Program_____ 39

Chapter 4 Tiny BASIC Specification _____ 42

Definitions: _____ 42

Tiny BASIC Commands _____ 43

Tiny BASIC Statements_____ 43

Operational Features _____ 44

Chapter 5 Tiny BASIC Design _____ 46

Tiny BASIC's Flow_____ 46

Tiny BASIC's Structure _____ 46

Tiny BASIC's Modularity _____ 48

Chapter 6 Editor/Command Mode _____ 51

Setup Code _____ 51

Main Loop 1 Code _____ 53

*Chapter 7 Execution Mode*_____ 58

Main Loop 2 Code _____ 59

*Chapter 8 Tiny BASIC Commands*_____ 63

NEW Command _____ 63

LIST Command _____ 64

RUN Command_____ 66

LOAD Command_____ 66

Chapter 9 LET Statement _____ 71

Expression Subroutine_____ 71

LET Statement _____ 79

*Chapter 10 INPUT and PRINT Statements*_____ 81

PRINT Statement _____ 82

Chapter 11 GOTO and IF..THEN Statements _____ 87

GOTO Statement _____ 87

IF Statement _____ 89

Chapter 12 – GOSUB/RETURN, STOP, and REM Statements _____ *94*

GOSUB and RET (Return) Statements_____ 94

STOP Statement_____ 95

REM Statement _____ 95

*Chapter 13 Testing Tiny BASIC*_____ *97*

Chapter 14 Tiny BASIC Extended (TBX) _____ *99*

Preprocessing Program Lines _____ 99

Multi-Statement Lines_____ 102

Data Arrays _____ 105

Logical Expression Evaluation _____ 108

IF...THEN Extension _____ 110

RPT – Repeat Statement _____ 112

Data Statement _____ 114

Chapter 15 Adding TBX Keywords _____ *118*

Modifying Keyword Tables _____ 118

Adding New Statement POKE _____ 121

Adding New Function PEEK _____ 121

Chapter 16 Testing TBX _____ *124*

Improved Readability _____ 124

Improved Speed _____ 125

Conway's Game of Life _____ 125

*Chapter 17 FPGA Implementation*_____ *132*

ZOC Terminal Emulator _____ 132

BYOC-24 CPU _____ 134

Preloaded TBX Programs _____ 139

Save/Load Programs with ZOC _____ 140

Chapter 18 Conclusion _____ 143

Appendix A BYOC-24 CPU Instruction Set _____ 144

Appendix B High/Low Guessing Game _____ 147

Appendix C Data RAM Storage _____ 152

Appendix D Tiny BASIC Subroutine Library _____ 153

Appendix E Random Number Generator _____ 158

Appendix F Logisim Debugger _____ 160

Appendix G Tiny BASIC Development Cycle _____ 163

Preface

In my first book in this series, "Build Your Own Computer-From Scratch", I started with a few basic concepts and guided the nontechnical reader through the design of a working computer. The emphasis was on hardware design with less attention paid to software.

In this book, software is the focus. As before, I make no assumptions regarding your technical knowledge of computers. I start with a few basic concepts and build a version of the BASIC programming language. To test Tiny BASIC, we use the BYOC-24 CPU, a modified version of the computer design introduced in my first book. We first test Tiny BASIC on a simulated BYOC-24 CPU using the freeware application Logisim. Later, we make Tiny BASIC fully functional using an Intel Cyclone V field programmable gate array.

Given this brief introduction to computer language design, I believe you will be encouraged to explore other areas of computing. At the very least, I hope you will appreciate more fully what happens when you type "RUN", "COMPILE", or press the green "GO" button in whatever computer language you use.

Chapter 1
Computer Programs

Computer Languages

A *computer program* is a collection of instructions that, when executed by a computer, performs a given task. Instructions come in various formats. At the computer hardware level, instructions are given in *machine language* made up of digital 0s and 1s. Each *instruction word* tells the computer to perform a single operation such as moving data or making a calculation.

Machine language, with its combination of 1s and 0s, is not easy for humans to understand and use. Instead, we prefer languages that are more meaningful. The "lowest" of these is *assembly language* that directly associates machine instructions with more easily understood abbreviated words and symbols. A software program called an *assembler* translates assembly instructions into machine language that executes on the computer.

Assembly language gives us the greatest control over the computer's operation, but it is very detailed and tedious to use. For this reason, higher level languages have been created that come closer to human language. Some of these like C++ and Java are used by professional programmers. Others, like BASIC, are directed at beginners and serve a more recreational purpose. The BASIC language has a long history of use as an introduction to programming that dates back to 1964 when it was developed by John G. Kemeny and Thomas E. Kurtz at Dartmouth College. Its English-like instructions and ease of use account for its early popularity in the history of personal computing.

Tiny BASIC is a dialect of BASIC that originated in Bob Albrecht's "The People's Computer Company Newsletter" back in the mid-1970's. I wrote the first published version back then. It ran in 1 kilobyte of memory on an Altair 8800 computer, one of the first personal computers. While Tiny BASIC was very limited in features, it performed many of the basic functions of a high-level language and, more importantly, was readily implementable in Intel 8080 machine language. Yes, I wrote in machine language, as an assembler was not available to me in those very early days of personal computing!

To better illustrate the differences between low- and high-level languages, consider this simple High/Low Guessing Game. In the game, we ask the player to guess a secret number. With each guess, we inform the player whether it is "Too high" or "Too low". The object of the game is to guess the secret number in the fewest number of tries. Here is dialog from a typical game.

```
High/Low Guessing Game

I am thinking of a number between 1 and 100.
Your guess ?50
Too high.  Try again.
Your guess ?25
Too low. Try again
Your guess ?37
Too high.  Try again.
Your guess ?31
Too high.  Try again.
Your guess ?28
Too high.  Try again.
Your guess ?27
You got it in  6 tries
```

In assembly language, this is the code needed to print the title and instruction lines.

```
setup:    lxi    irom,msg0     ;Display title message
          call   mout
;
;  Main Routine
;
main:     call   new_line      ;Skip line
          call   new_line
          lxi    irom,msg1     ;Display instructions
          call   mout
          call   new_line      ;Next line
. . .
new_line: mvi e,eol            ;Load E with new line character
```

```
            jmp eout            ;Display it
. . .
mout:       ldx    e,irom       ;Get character from Data ROM
            or     e,e          ;Is it zero?
            rz                  ;If so, done
            call   eout         ;If not, display it
            inx    irom         ;Point to next character
            jmp    mout         ;Do again
. . .
msg0:       ds     High/Low Guessing Game
msg1:       ds     I am thinking of a number between 1 and 100.
```

In Tiny BASIC, the same task is performed with these instructions.

```
10 PRINT "High/Low Guessing Game":PRINT:PRINT
20 PRINT "I am thinking of a number between 1 and 100.":PRINT
```

The most striking difference is in the number of lines of code, 17 versus 2. The assembly language version of the complete game requires more than 200 lines of code while in Tiny BASIC, only 18 lines are needed! That's a 10 to 1 difference! Also, the Tiny BASIC version is much easier to understand because it is self-documenting. The assembly version, on the other hand, requires detailed annotation.

What's not as obvious, is the difference in development process. The assembly version must be edited with a text editor program, assembled with a special program, then loaded into computer's memory before it can be executed. To make even the simplest change, the whole time consuming process must be repeated. Tiny BASIC, on the other hand, has a built-in text editor and executes directly from the program text by simply entering the RUN command.

This direct execution of program text classifies Tiny BASIC as an *interpretive language*. In the old days, when computers were much slower, the processing overhead with interpreters made them slow and less desirable for professional use. As computer speeds increased, this became less of an issue and interpreters became a mainstay of modern computers. Java, perhaps the most popular language today, is an interpreter. Others include Python and Perl. Learn more at https://en.wikipedia.org/wiki/Interpreted_language.

BASIC is clearly a beginner's language and has its shortcomings. Among them, its "GOTO" statement encourages unstructured coding that can produce confusing and error prone programs. Nevertheless, its simplicity and ease of use encourages new comers to experiment and learn the basics of programming.

Language Design

Quality computer programs, whether in low or high level languages, have certain recognizable characteristics. Among these are program flow, structure, and modularity.

Flow

Program flow relates to the order a program executes, which, in general, is one instruction executing after another. Some instructions exercise *flow control* within the program, either executing different code depending on a condition or repeating code segments in what we call a *loop*. The diagram below illustrates a traditional flow pattern alongside a modern one.

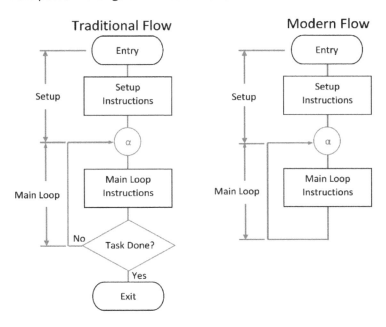

With traditional flow, once the program task is completed, the program exits.[i] Modern programs for personal computers execute without exiting, waiting always for user interaction to select and perform tasks. Notice also that, in both cases, the flow pattern divides into two sections, "Setup" and "Main Loop".

Structure

Programs make use of three logic structures: sequence, selection, and repetition. Each has a specific function as the computer carries out the program task.

Let's examine the High/Low Guessing Game to identify these logic structures. The game's flow pattern and structure are best illustrated with a *functional flowchart*.

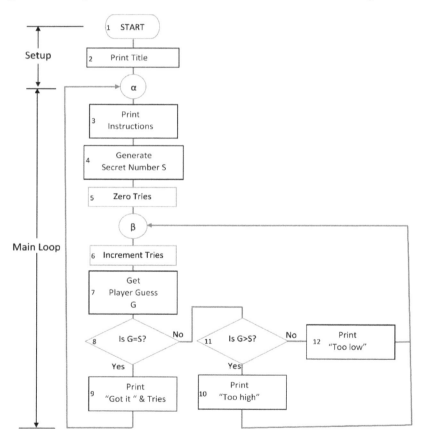

In a functional flowchart, blocks represent steps in playing the game including their order and any decision points encountered along the way. The arrangement of blocks, in turn, exhibits structure as described below.

Sequence Structure

Sequence structure is the simplest structure consisting of a series of process blocks with no decision making or branching. In the flowchart, the code segment consisting of blocks 3 to 6 is an example of sequence structure.

Selection Structure

The diamond shapes in the flowchart represent *selection structure* where branching occurs based on a condition, usually a "yes/no" or "true/false" result. In the flowchart, block 9 checks if the player's guess G is equal to the secret number R. If "true" the game is won and the game restarts. Block 11 modifies the flow depending on whether the guess is too high or low.

Repetition Structure

Repetition structure is exemplified by sections of a program that repeat. Repeating sections are called *loops*. In the flowchart, there are two loops. The inner loop that repeats at junction "β" takes the player's guesses until the secret number is guessed. The outer loop at junction "α" starts a new game.

The "modern flow pattern" is easily recognized including the "Setup" and never-ending "Main Loop". Notice also that the inner loop does not overlap the "Main Loop". This is a critical design constraint that prevents confusing "spaghetti code".

Modularity

Program modularity involves dividing the program into separate functioning modules that combine to complete the required task. Modular programming has several advantages. First, modules that perform specific tasks tend to be less complicated and therefore easier to understand and code. Second, because they are narrowly purposed, modules are less error prone and easier to debug should an error occur. Third, modules are reusable; that is, when a task is required at several points in a program, a single module can be accessed at each point, thus avoiding code duplication.

Modules of a general type may be usable across programs, giving rise to *module libraries*. Modern languages come with extensive libraries that are excellent resources for program development. An important point is that we don't have to know how library programs work to use them.

Modules come in a variety of types. The two principal types are *functions* and *subroutines*. Functions perform a single action and can return a value. Subroutines perform a specific task and generally do not return a value. Functions and subroutines can appear anywhere in a program including within other functions and subroutines.

We focus on subroutines because they play a prominent role in both assembly and Tiny BASIC programming. As an example, consider the block in the High/Low Guessing Game flowchart the prints the title. Technically, the block is called a *process block*. Printing messages is a common task in programming of all types, so it lends itself to modularization. When converting a functional flowchart to a programming flowchart, we change such process blocks to *predefined process blocks*. See the figure below.

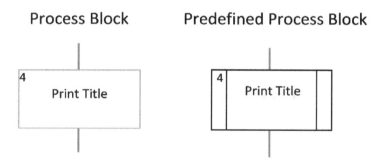

Process Block   Predefined Process Block

At coding time, predefined process blocks are coded as functions or subroutines.

In summary, here are the design elements we will use in programming.

1. The body of the program will consist of a "Setup" code segment followed by a "Main Loop" segment.
2. Program logic will consist of sequence, selection, and repetition structural types.

3. No repetition loops will overlap.
4. When modularity is appropriate, subroutines will be used.

Now that we have a good idea of how our programs should look, we can move on to implementing the High/Low Guessing Game in BYOC-24 Assembly Language.

Chapter 2
The BYOC-24 CPU

In this chapter, we describe the BYOC-24 CPU and introduce the machine instructions that are the basis for its assembly language. In my book, "Build Your Own Computer – From Scratch" book, I describe the design of a computer called the BYOC CPU. The BYOC-24 CPU is 24-bit variation of that design with features that facilitate programming Tiny BASIC. See particularly specification 5 below.

BYOC-24 CPU Specification

Listed below are the basic specifications for the BYOC-24 CPU.

1. Program Memory: 65 kilobytes, 24-bit wide RAM (Random Access Memory) [ii].

2. Data Memory: Data RAM, 65 kilobytes, 8-bit wide; Data ROM, 65 kilobytes, 8-bit wide[iii].

3. Eight 8-bit general purpose registers designated A, B, C, D, E, H, L, M. M is a special register that indirectly addresses any location in Data RAM. It uses the pairing of the H and L registers as a 16-bit address pointer. M adds the functionality of the other registers to memory locations specified by the address in HL.

4. An 8-bit arithmetic-logic unit (ALU) capable of basic arithmetic operations (addition and subtraction), logical operations (AND, OR, NOT, and XOR), and register manipulation including right and left bit rotation.

5. Indirect Data Access: Two 16-bit index registers, IRAM, an address pointer into Data RAM, and IROM, an address pointer into Data ROM. For programming Tiny BASIC, IRAM is used as the address pointer to the Tiny BASIC program stored in Data RAM. IROM is used to access Tiny BASIC related tables and messages stored in the Data ROM.

Note: The one area of Tiny BASIC coding that is not 8-bit is arithmetic calculation. In this case, we use 16-bit, signed binary numbers providing a numeric range of -32,768 to +32,767. Register pairs (like HL and DE) and two 8-bit RAM locations are used to handle these 16-bit values.

BYOC-24 Instruction Set

In the section, we briefly explore the BYOC-24 instruction set. As already mentioned, my book, "Build Your Own Computer – From Scratch" has a more comprehensive treatment of machine and assembly language for the BYOC family of CPUs. What we include here provides enough background for the undertaking ahead.

BYOC-24 instructions tell the computer what to do. They are primitive in comparison to Tiny BASIC statements and commands. It often takes hundreds of bytes of machine code to execute a single Tiny BASIC statement. Were it not for the speed of modern CPU's, this processing time would make interpreters like Tiny BASIC impractical. But, at millions of instructions per second, we are never aware of the added execution processing time.

The BYOC-24 is classified as an 8-bit CPU because its instructions are optimized to process the 8-bit words that make up Tiny BASIC programs. Take for instance, this line from a Tiny BASIC program.

10 let a=0

This is how it would look as entered from the keyboard:

ASCII Codes (in 8-bit binary) ->
00110001 00110000 00100000 01101100 01100101 01110100 00100000 01100001 00110001 0011000 00001101
  "1"   "0"   " "   "l"   "e"   "t"   " "   "a"   "="   "0"   CR

Each byte is a 6-bit ASCII code[iv] prefixed by two 0 bits to make an 8-bit word. The first two bytes are the line number followed by the remaining characters in the line. The ASCII control character CR ("Carriage Return"), is used to indicate the end of the program line.

After pre-processed and stored in Data RAM, it looks like this.

```
ASCII Characters ------------>   "l"      "e"      "t"      " "      "a"      "="      "0"      CR
00000000 00001010 00001001 01101100 01100101 01110100 00100000 01100001 00110001 0011000 00001101
|   Line Number  | | Length |
```

The first two bytes are the 16-bit binary equivalent of the line number. The third byte is the line length measured from the current position to and including the CR byte. The remaining ASCII characters fill out the line. In its final form, the program line consists of 8-bit words in Data RAM.

Thus, from first inputting text from the keyboard to pre-processing the program line, great advantage is gained using a CPU with instructions designed to work efficiently with 8-bit words.

The BYOC-24 instruction set as describe below is divided into seven categories based on shared functionality. Further, assembly language mnemonics are used rather than 24-bit machine language. A more detailed listing can be found in Appendix A.

These abbreviations apply to the instruction descriptions.

r_d, r_s	Register Code:
	0b000 M 0b001 L 0b010 H 0b011 E 0b100 D 0b101 C 0b110 B 0b111 A
Z	Zero status bit, set or reset depending on a arithmetic or logic operation
C	Carry status bit, set or reset depending on an arithmetic operation
V	8-bit constant value
V	16-bit constant value
a	MS Byte "11111111" LS Byte "aaaaaaaa" (0b00000000 to 0b11111111)
A	16-bit address
P	8-bit I/O port address
{..}	{Status Bits Affected}

Note: A "0x" prefix indicates a hexadecimal (base 16) value. A "0b" prefix indicates a binary (base 2) value. 0s and 1s within quotes indicates a binary value (base 2) value.

1. Register Operations
These instructions move data into and among registers.

MVI r_d,V   Move value to register
MOV r_d,r_s Move register r_s to r_d
MOV r_d,IRAML Move index register IRAM$_{0-7}$ to r_d
MOV r_d,IRAMH Move index register IRAM$_{8-15}$ to r_d
MOV r_d,IROML Move index register IROM$_{0-7}$ to r_d
MOV r_d,IROMH Move index register IROM$_{8-15}$ to r_d

Examples:
MVI B,100 – Moves the decimal value 100 to register B
MOV A,B – Moves the contents of the B register to register A
MOV L,IRAML – Moves the LS 8 bits of the index register to register L
 MOV H,IRAMH - Moves the MS 8 bits of the index register to register L

Note: "LS" and "MS" stand for "Least Significant" and "Most Significant",
respectively.   255 is the largest number an 8-bit register can hold.

2. Data RAM and ROM Access

These instructions provide read and write access (as appropriate) to the BYOC-24's
Data RAM and Data ROM.

LDR r_d,a   Load register r_d direct from Data RAM address 1..1a..a
STR A,r_s Store register r_s direct at Data RAM address 1..1a..a
LDX r_d,(IRAM)   Load register r_d indirect from Data RAM address in IRAM
LDX r_d,(IROM)   Load register r_d indirect from Data ROM address in IROM
STX (IRAM), r_s Store register r_s indirect at Data RAM address in IRAM

Note: LDR and STR instructions load and store values in the upper 256 bytes of the
Data RAM; i.e., 0xFF00 to 0xFFFF. A "0x" prefix indicates a hexadecimal (base 16)
value.

Examples:
LDR D,10 – Loads register D with the contents of memory at address 0xff0A.
LDX D,(IRAM) – Loads D register with contents of Data RAM address in IRAM.
LDX C,(IROM) – Loads C register with the contents of Data ROM address in IROM.
STX (IRAM),C – Stores contents of register C in Data RAM at address in IRAM.

Note: If IROM is 0xFF0A, the LDR D,10 and LDX D,(IROM) produce identical results.

3. Index Register Operations

These instructions provide access to the index registers IRAM and IROM.

LDHL IRAM	Load Data RAM index register IRAM with HL
ADHL IRAM	Add HL to Data RAM index register IRAM
CPHL IRAM	Compare Data RAM index register IRAM to HL {C,Z}
INX IRAM	Increment Data RAM index register IRAM
DCX IRAM	Decrement Data RAM index register IRAM
LDHL IROM	Load Data ROM index register IROM with HL
ADHL IROM	Add HL to Data ROM index register IROM
CPHL IROM	Compare Data RAM index register IROM to HL {C,Z}
INX IROM	Increment Data ROM index register IROM
DCX IROM	Decrement Data ROM index register IROM
LXI IRAM,V	Load Data RAM index register IRAM immediate
LXI IROM,V	Load Data ROM index register IROM immediate
CPI IRAM,V	Compare Data RAM index register IRAM immediate {C,Z}
CPI IROM,V	Compare Data ROM index register IROM immediate {C,Z}

Examples:
LHLD IRAM – If HL is 0x3010, then IRAM is 0x3010 after execution
ADHL IRAM – If HL=0x0100 and IRAM=0x0400, the IRAM is 0x0500 after execution.
CPHL IRAM – If IROM=0x1000 and HL=0x1000, the Z="1" and C="0" after execution.
INX IROM – If IROM=0x0105, then IROM is 0x0106 after execution.
LXI IROM,0x1000 – IROM is 0x1000 after execution.
CPI IROM,0x0100 – If IROM=0x0020, then Z="0" (not zero) and C="1" (with carry)

4. Arithmetic/Logic Operations

These instructions perform arithmetic and logical operations using the 8-bit registers.

ADD r_d,r_s	Add registers: $r_d + r_s$ → r_d & {C,Z}
SUB r_d,r_s	Subtract registers: $r_d - r_s$ → r_d {C,Z}
ADC r_d,r_s	Add registers w/ carry: $r_d + r_s + c$ → r_d {C,Z}
SBB r_d,r_s	Subtract registers w/ borrow: $r_d - r_s - b$ → r_d {C,Z

AND r_d,r_s	AND registers: r_d AND r_s → r_d {Z,C=0}
OR r_d,r_s	OR registers: r_d OR r_s → r_d {Z,C=0}
XOR r_d,r_s	XOR registers: r_d XOR r_s → r_d {Z,C=0}
NOT r_d,r_s	Invert register: NOT r_s → r_d {Z,C=0}
ADI r_d,V	Add immediate to register: r_d + V → r_d {C,Z}
SUI r_d,V	Subtr immediate from register: r_d - V → r_d {C,Z}
ACI r_d,V	Add immediate to register w/ carry: r_d + V + c → r_d {C,Z}
SBI r_d,V	Subtr immediate from register w/ borrow: r_d - V - b → r_d {C,Z}
ANI r_d,V	AND immediate register r_d AND V → r_d {Z,C=0}
ORI r_d,V	OR immediate register: r_d OR V → r_d {Z,C=0}
XRI r_d,V	XOR immediate register: r_d XOR V → r_d {Z,C=0}
NTI r_d,V	Invert immediate: NOT V → r_d {Z,C=0}
RLC r_d	Rotate register left: C <- 7..0 <- 0 {C}
RRC r_d	Rotate register right: 0 -> 7..0 -> C {C}
RAL r_d	Rotate register left through carry: C <- 7..0 <- 0 {C}
RAR r_d	Rotate register right through carry: C -> 7..0 -> {C}
INR r_d	Increment register r_d: r_d + 1 -> r_d {Z }
DCR r_d	Decrement register r_d: r_d - 1 -> r_d {Z}
STC	Set carry {C}
CMP r_d,r_s	Subtract registers: r_d - r_s; r_d → r_d {Z,C}
CPI r_d,V	Subtr immediate from register: r_d – V; → r_d {Z,C}

Examples: Assume A=0b00001001 B=0b00000111 C=0b11111101
SUI B,0x40 – B=0xC7 {C="1" Z="0"} after execution.
CPI B,0x40 – {C="1" Z="0"} after execution. B unchanged.
ADD A,B – A=0b00010000 after execution. B unchanged.
AND A,B – If {C="1"} before, then A=0b00000001 and {C="0" Z="0"} after.
XOR B,C – B=0b11111010 after execution. C unchanged.
RRC B – B=0b00000011 {C="1" Z unaffected}
INR C – C=0b11111110 {C unaffected, Z="0"} after execution.

5. Miscellaneous Operations

This category is a catch-all for special instructions.

External Input/Output

Computer need the ability to interact with the outside world. The BYOC-24 CPU uses the INP and OUT instructions for this purpose. They provide access to external Input/Output ports that, in turn, communicate with the outside world. In the Logisim version, a keyboard input port and a TTY (display) output port are incorporated in the design. The Cyclone V FPGA version includes a serial I/O port to communicate with an external terminal with keyboard and display.

INP r_d,P   Input from I/O port P to destination register r_d
OUT P,r_s Output to I/O port P from source register r_s

The "INP r_d,P" instruction reads input port P and stores the 8-bit value in destination register r_d. The "OUT P,r_s" instruction sends the value in source register r_s to output port P.

PUSH/POP Memory Stack

PUSH and POP instructions use a first in/last out memory stack to save and restore register values. The PUSH/POP (PP) Stack is a separate RAM memory that can store up to 255 8-bit values. Only the value of a register is saved on the stack. For example, PUSH A followed later by POP B updates B with the pushed value A. When using multiple PUSHs and POPs, the last value pushed is the first popped. For instance, to save both registers A and B, we would first PUSH A, then PUSH B. To restore them, we POP B first, then POP A. And finally, for every PUSH there must be a POP. Failure to keep up with PUSHs and POPs results in programming errors.

PUSHs and POPs are valuable for saving and restoring values in coding complex tasks that use all the CPU's registers. They also are used to pass data to and return results from subroutines This latter use features prominently in our coding that evaluates Tiny BASIC expressions.

POP r_d Pop top of PP Stack to register r_d
PUSH r_s Push register r_s on top of PP Stack

Example: This is code from the High/Low Guessing Game that outputs a character to the Logisim display.

```
;
; Print Single Character in A
;
chrout:         push      a                     ;Save A
chrout0:        inp       a,cntrport            ;Print device busy?
                ani       a,0b10000000
                jnz       chrout0               ;If so, wait
                pop       a                     ;Restore a
                out       dataport,a            ;Print character
                ret                             ;Done and return
      . . .
cntrport        equ                           0 ;Terminal Unit control/status port
dataport        equ                           1 ;Terminal Unit data port
```

Note: The BYOC assembler is not case sensitive, so "out dataport,a" is the same as "OUT DATAPORT,A". Using all lower case with the text editor (Notepad++ is our preference)) makes typing easier.

When the subroutine is called, the character to be output is in the A register. Because we use register A to check the display busy status bit on the control port (cntrport), we must first save the display character with a "push a" instruction and restore it later with a "pop a" for outputting.

6. Subroutines

In order to support modular programming, the BYOC-24 CPU provides the "CALL" instruction and a collection of return instructions "RET", "RZ", "RNZ", "RC", and "RNC". At any point in the program, a CALL can be inserted to perform a predefined process task. "Th CALL label" instruction transfers to the subroutine at address "label". Subroutines may contain additional CALLs, referred to as "nested" CALLs. The RET instruction is unconditional while the remaining variations are conditioned on zero and carry status bit values. For instance, RZ returns from a subroutine if the zero-status bit is "1" at that point. Return instructions transfer execution back to the instruction immediately following the original call.

CALL/RET instructions use the first in/last out CR Stack. The CR Stack is composed of a 256 byte 16-bit RAM that allows up to 255 levels of CALLs, more than enough for our purposes.

In general, we always exit a subroutine with a return instruction. Otherwise, we leave trash addresses on the CR Stack. A rare exception is processing error conditions, in which case, we must reset the stack pointer. See the "Main Loop 1" discussion in Chapter 6.

CALL A   Call subroutine at address A
RET   Return from subroutine
RZ   Return from subroutine on zero
RNZ   Return from subroutine on not zero
RC   Return from subroutine on carry
RNC   Return from subroutine on not carry

Example: The message output subroutine in the High/Low Guessing Game is a good example of how a subroutine is used. Printing text messages is done in several places in the program, so the "msgout" subroutine saves duplication of code. It also demonstrates calling a subroutine within a subroutine and using a conditional return, RZ.

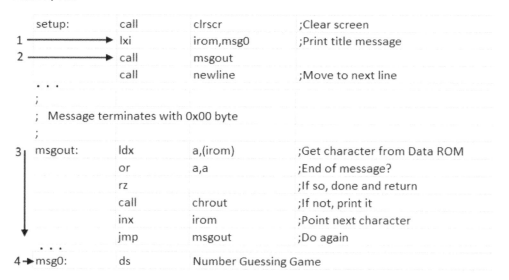

```
      setup:        call      clrscr          ;Clear screen
1 ───────────►     lxi       irom,msg0       ;Print title message
2 ───────────►     call      msgout
                   call      newline         ;Move to next line
      . . .
      ;
      ;  Message terminates with 0x00 byte
      ;
3 ┐   msgout:       ldx       a,(irom)        ;Get character from Data ROM
  │                 or        a,a             ;End of message?
  │                 rz                        ;If so, done and return
  │                 call      chrout          ;If not, print it
  │                 inx       irom            ;Point next character
  ▼                 jmp       msgout          ;Do again
      . . .
4 ──► msg0:         ds        Number Guessing Game
```

1. Messages like the game's title are stored in the BYOC-24's Data ROM. Label "msg0" is the address of the title message in Data ROM. The first step in printing

the message is to point index register IROM to "msg0" using the load index register immediate "LXI" instruction.

2. We call the message output subroutine "msgout" with the message address in IROM.

3. We store the title message in Data ROM as ASCII characters ending with a 0x00 byte. In this code segment, we scan the message printing each character until reaching the ending 0x00 byte. We use the load indirect from index register "LDX A,(IROM)" to load register A with the byte at the address in index register IROM. The parentheses around IROM reminds us that this is an indirect load; i.e., we are not loading A with IROM but with the byte at the address in IROM.

The "OR A,A" is a clever way to detect the zero end byte 0x00. ORing a register with itself has no effect on the value in A but it updates the zero-status bit. At message end, the zero-status byte triggers the RZ instruction returning execution to the calling program. Until the 0x00 byte is reached, we fall through RZ, output the character, increment IROM, and loop back to get the next byte.

4. ASCII message "msg0" is the Data portion of the source code and assembles into the Data ROM. As usual, the label "msg0" must be in column 1 followed by a colon. "DS" (meaning define string) is in the second column and the message is in the third column. The 0x00 end byte is added automatically by the assembler.

7. Jumping and Branching

Jumping and branching instructions change the executing address. We use them when implementing selection and repetition structure. The jump instructions JMP and PCHL unconditionally change the executing address and have only a narrow range of uses that we explore in detail later.

The conditional jumps or branching instructions(JZ, JNZ, JC, and JNC) are more common and change the executing address based on zero and carry status bits.

JMP A	Jump to address a…a
PCHL	Jump to address in HL
JZ A	Jump on zero to address a…a
JNZ A	Jump on not zero to address a…a
JC A	Jump on carry to address a…a

JNC A   Jump on not carry to address a...a

Examples:

JMP MAIN   After execution, executing address is changed to the 16-bit value MAIN.

PCHL   If HL=0x0100, then executing address changes to 0x0100.

JZ REDO   If the zero status is "1", the executing address changes to the 16-bit
             value represented by label REDO. If the zero status is "0", the jump is
             ignored and execution continues at the next instruction.

This completes our description of the BYOC-24 CPU and its instruction set. In the
next chapter, we look at BYOC-24 assembly language in greater detail.

Chapter 3
Assembly Language

As already noted, assembly code replaces machine instructions with English-like abbreviated words and symbols that are easier to remember and use. For instance, to load the A register with constant value 10, this is the assembly code.

"MVI A,10"

The equivalent machine code looks like this.

"000 111 00 0000 0000 00001010"

Clearly, assembly is easier to understand and use. Still, programming in assembly is detailed and tedious. A good way to address this is the use of a subroutine library.

Subroutine Libraries

Using a subroutine library, complex and duplicative tasks are preprogrammed so that the programmer can focus on higher level and often simpler tasks. To illustrate, we use this approach below to program the High/Low Guessing Game. Later, we will use a subroutine library to develop Tiny BASIC.

We start with the previously developed functional flowchart for the High/Low Guessing Game.

(Next page please)

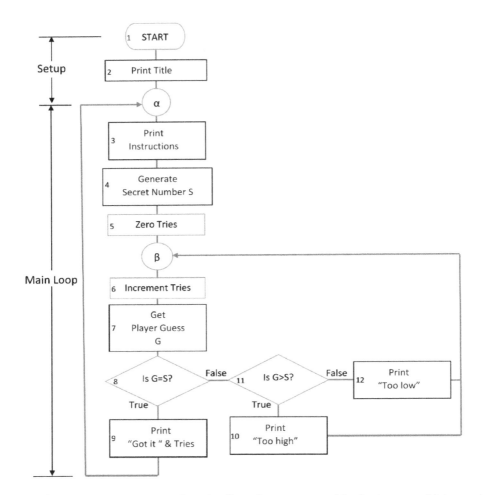

For the next step, we examine the flowchart process blocks to see which can be replaced with predefined process blocks. As a basis, we ask two questions about each block. First, do multiple instances of the same or similar blocks appear in the flowchart? Second, does the block perform a complex task that cannot be performed by a simple and short sequence of assembly instructions.

Answering these questions for the High/Low Guessing Game flowchart, we identify and convert process blocks to predefined process blocks as noted below.

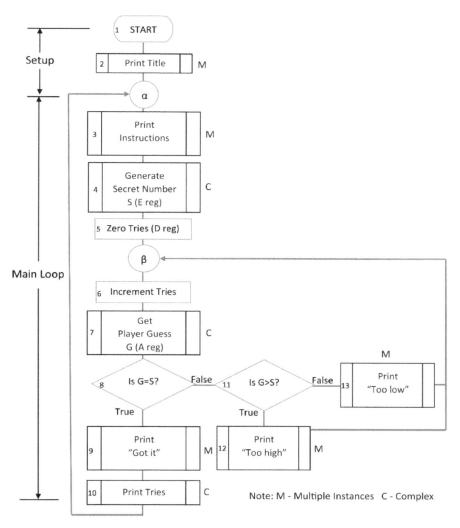

1. We replace "Print" process blocks (2,3,,9,10,12, and 13) by predefined process blocks because they appear multiple times in the flowchart.
2. The "Print Got it & Tries" process block was split into two predefined process blocks because printing text and printing a number are different tasks.
3. The "Generate Secret Number" process block (4) was replaced by a predefined process block because it performs a complex task.
4. The "Get Player Guess" process block (7) was replaced by a predefined process

block because it performs a complex task.

5. The remaining process blocks represent tasks that can be performed with a simple sequence of assembly instructions.

6. Because there are so few variables, we have pre-assigned BYOC-24 CPU registers A, D, and E as shown.

Note: To assign a register to a program variable, the maximum value must be 255 or less. Large and complex programs like Tiny BASIC involve so many variables and of so many sizes that assigning registers at this stage would not be possible.

Predefined process blocks in the flowchart become library subroutines for us to use when coding the game. For the High/Low Guessing Game, these are the library subroutines.

1. Print Message Subroutine (multiple instances)
2. Get Secret Number Subroutine (complex task)
3. Get Player Guess Subroutine (complex task)
4. Print Number Subroutine (complex task)

For this and Tiny BASIC later, the library subroutines will have been coded and are ready to use. To use them, we need only specify this information:

"Name" – Subroutine name
"In" – Information/data passed either directly or indirectly to the subroutine when called
"Out" – Information/data passed back either directly or indirectly upon return from the subroutine
 "Reg Used" – Registers used by the subroutine
 "Description" – A description of what the subroutine does.

Note: "Reg Used" lets us know that the registers listed are subject to change by the subroutine and should be saved by the calling routine. Otherwise, a programming error would occur.

High/Low Guessing Game Library
The following subroutines make up the High/Low Guessing Game Library:

msgout – {In: IROM=starting address of ASCII message in Data ROM; Out: None; Reg Used: A and IROM} Prints the ASCII text starting at the address in IROM and ending when a 0x00 end byte is encountered.

Note: This is an example of passing data indirectly, as the data is not the IROM, but the data pointed to by the address in IROM.

getrndm– {In: None; Out: E = pseudo-random number 0 to 100; Reg Used: A, E, and IROM} Prints message requesting player strike any key at some random time. The code reads an 8-bit counter counting at the CPU's clock rate. The result in the range of 0 to 255 is transformed with a modulo operation to the range of 0 to 100 and returned in E.

getguess – {In: None; Out: A = player's guess; Reg Used: A, C, H, and L} Takes player's guess entered on the keyboard and returns it in register A.

printnum – {In: D=number to print; Out: None; Reg Used: A, C, H, and L} Print the unsigned number from 0 to 255 in register D.

Note: This is an example of passing data directly, as the data is in register D.

Although not included in the flowchart, two additional subroutines are available for print formatting.

clrscr – {In: None; Out: None; Reg Used: A} Outputs clear screen byte(s) to the display device.

newline – {In: None; Out: None; Reg Used: A} Skips to the next line on the display device.

The source code for these subroutines can be found in Appendix B. Keep in mind that we don't have to know how they work if we have the library information documented above.

The "Setup" Code Segment

Given access to the High/Low Guessing Game Library, we can focus on the remaining process blocks in the flowchart. We begin with the "Setup" section.

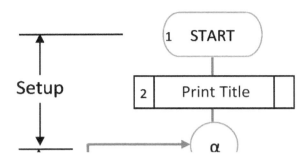

Block 1 – Print Title

"Start" is the entry point of the program. For the BYOC-24 CPU, it is always address 0x0000. In the "Stop" mode, performing a system reset loads the program counter with 0x0000. Enabling the "Run" mode starts execution at 0x0000.

Block 2 – Print Title

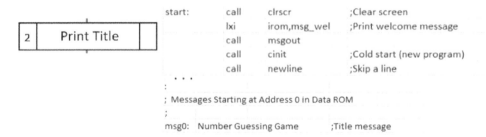

We clear the display by calling library subroutine "scrclr". Before calling "msgout", we use the LXI instruction to load IROM with the title message's address "msg0". We then call "msgout" and follow up with "newline" to skip to the next line. This completes the "Setup" code.

The "Main Loop" Segment

The "Main Loop" section of the High/Low Guessing Game flowchart is shown below.

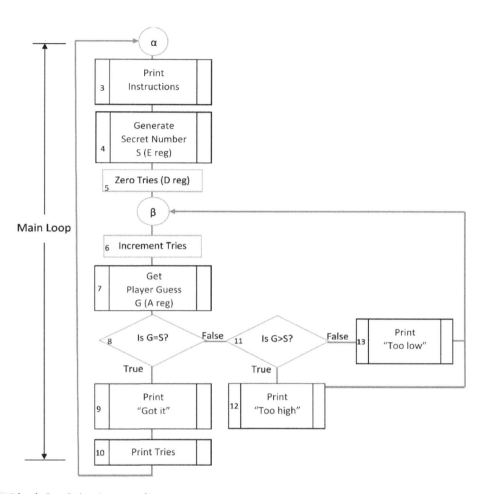

Block 3 – Print Instructions

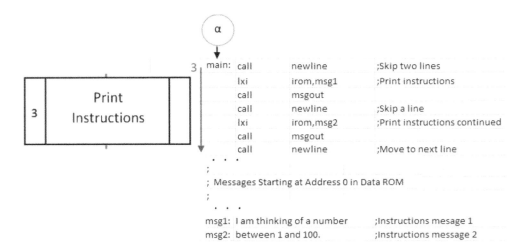

```
              3 | main:  call        newline         ;Skip two lines
                        lxi         irom,msg1       ;Print instructions
                        call        msgout
                        call        newline         ;Skip a line
                        lxi         irom,msg2       ;Print instructions continued
                        call        msgout
                        call        newline         ;Move to next line
                .  .  .
                ;
                ; Messages Starting at Address 0 in Data ROM
                ;
                .  .  .
                msg1:  I am thinking of a number    ;Instructions mesage 1
                msg2:  between 1 and 100.           ;Instructions message 2
```

The "main" label marks the point where a new game starts. In order to leave space after the title, we call "newline" again. We then load IROM with "msg1" and call "msgout" to print the first instruction line. We follow with "newline" to move to the next line and call "msgout" again, this time with IROM pointing to "msg2", the second line of instructions. Finally, a "newline" skips to the next line.

Block 4 – Get Secret Number to be Guessed

```
              4  call        getrndm            ;Get secret number, E reg
```

All that's needed here is to call the random number library subroutine "getrndm". Register E returns with a secret number between 0 and 100.

Block 5 – Zero Tries

```
              5  mvi         d,0                ;Zero tries counter, D reg
```

The D register holds the number of tries. To zero it, we use the "MVI D,0" instruction.

Block 6 – New Guess Target and Increment Tries

| 6 | Increment Tries | | 6 guess: inr | d | ;Increment tries |

The "guess" label marks the point where a new guess starts. We use the INR instruction to increment (add 1 to) register D, the number of tries. Again, a process block is replaced with a simple instruction.

Block 7 – Get Player Guess

Here we use another straightforward call, this time to the "getguess" subroutine that returns the guess in register A.

Block 8 to Block 13 – Decision Blocks (See below.)

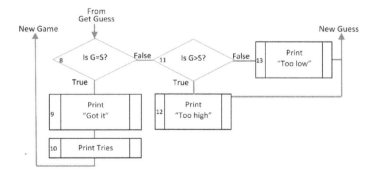

8	cmp	a,e	;Compare player's guess to secret number?
	jz	gotit	;If equal, branch to "Got It"
11	jnc	high	;If greater, branch to "high"
13	low: lxi	irom,msg7	;If less, print "Too Low" and do again
	call	msgout	
	jmp	guess	;Get another guess
	;		
12	high: lxi	irom,msg6	Print "Too High" message and do again
	call	msgout	
	jmp	guess	;Get another guess
	;		
9	gotit: lxi	irom,msg4	;Print "Got It" message and number tries
	call	msgout	
	mvi	l,0	;Don't print leading zeroes
10	call	printnum	;Print number of tries in D
	lxi	irom,msg5	
	call	msgout	
	jmp	main	;Do over from main entry point

Block 8 – Compare Player Guess to Secret Number and Process a Correct Guess

Register A contains the player's guess and register E, the secret number. The compare register "CMP A,E" instruction subtracts register E from register A but does not replace A with the difference as the SUB instruction would have done. CMP updates the zero and carry status bits as follows:

a. If A=E (i.e. Guess = Secret Number) then Z="1" and C="0"
b. If A>E (i.e. Guess > Secret Number) then Z="0" and C="0"
c. If A<E (i.e. Guess < Secret Number) then Z="0" and C="1"

We are ready to select the appropriate path with branching instructions. We first check for a correct guess (A=E and Z="1"). If true (condition "a" above), the jump-on-zero JZ instruction branches to the "gotit" code segment notifying the player the game is won.

Block 11 – Check for a High Guess
If condition "b" above is true, the player's guess is too high, and we branch to label "high" to process it.

Block 13 – Process Too Low Guess
If the comparison is not "a" or "b", then the condition "c" must be true, so we print a 'Too low' message and ask for another guess.

Block 12 – Process Too High Guess
We print a "Too high" message and ask for another guess.

Block 9-10 – Process Correct Guess and Print Tries
We print a "Got it" message. We print the number of tries by calling the library subroutine "printnum" then start a new game by jumping to label "main".

Below is the completed assembly version of the High/Low Guessing Game.

(Next page please)

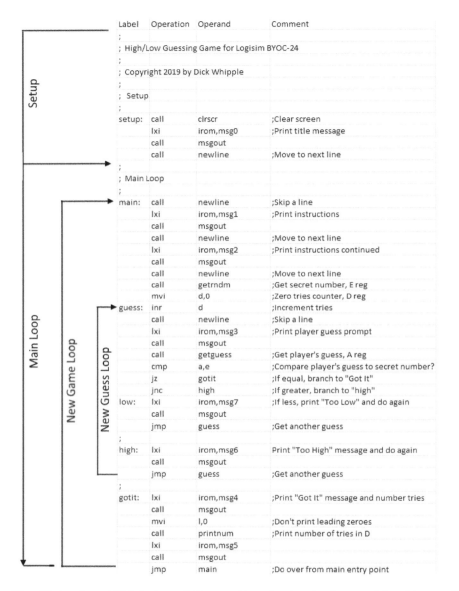

Label	Operation	Operand	Comment
;			
; High/Low Guessing Game for Logisim BYOC-24			
;			
; Copyright 2019 by Dick Whipple			
;			
; Setup			
;			
setup:	call	clrscr	;Clear screen
	lxi	irom,msg0	;Print title message
	call	msgout	
	call	newline	;Move to next line
;			
; Main Loop			
;			
main:	call	newline	;Skip a line
	lxi	irom,msg1	;Print instructions
	call	msgout	
	call	newline	;Move to next line
	lxi	irom,msg2	;Print instructions continued
	call	msgout	
	call	newline	;Move to next line
	call	getrndm	;Get secret number, E reg
	mvi	d,0	;Zero tries counter, D reg
guess:	inr	d	;Increment tries
	call	newline	;Skip a line
	lxi	irom,msg3	;Print player guess prompt
	call	msgout	
	call	getguess	;Get player's guess, A reg
	cmp	a,e	;Compare player's guess to secret number?
	jz	gotit	;If equal, branch to "Got It"
	jnc	high	;If greater, branch to "high"
low:	lxi	irom,msg7	;If less, print "Too Low" and do again
	call	msgout	
	jmp	guess	;Get another guess
;			
high:	lxi	irom,msg6	Print "Too High" message and do again
	call	msgout	
	jmp	guess	;Get another guess
;			
gotit:	lxi	irom,msg4	;Print "Got It" message and number tries
	call	msgout	
	mvi	l,0	;Don't print leading zeroes
	call	printnum	;Print number of tries in D
	lxi	irom,msg5	
	call	msgout	
	jmp	main	;Do over from main entry point

The "Setup" and "Main Loop" flow pattern is clearly discernable. Also, notice that the "New Game" and "New Guess" loops do not overlap.

Testing an Assembly Program

The simplest way to test our program is to simulate the BYOC-24 CPU using Logisim. Logisim is a popular logic simulator with an easy-to-use graphical user interface that makes it the perfect tool for developing and testing logic devices and circuits. Logisim executable file can be downloaded free of charge from www.Sourceforge.net. Double click to launch.

Consider the figure below.

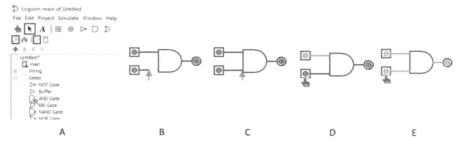

A   B   C   D   E

Logisim provides a workspace into which logic devices such as the AND gate in figure A can be dragged and dropped as in figure B. Logic inputs (small squares) and outputs (small circles) can be added to the design in a similar way. Wires connecting components can be added by dragging from contact to contact with the mouse and cursor as in figures B and C. A poke tool (small pointing finger) flips an input from "0" to "1" or vice versa. Note in figures D and E that changing the AND gate's second input to "1" causes the output to change to "1". Note also that dark green (or black) wires indicate a "0" logic level and bright green (or gray) wires indicate a "1" logic level.

Many video tutorials can be found on the internet. Most include helpful examples and cover troubleshooting techniques.

The Logisim circuit file for the BYOC-24 can be downloaded from http://github.com/rbwhipple/BYOC-24. The file you'll want is BYOC-24-Master.zip. After unzipping it, open the file BYOC-24-Hi-Lo.circ in Logisim and you should see this circuit.

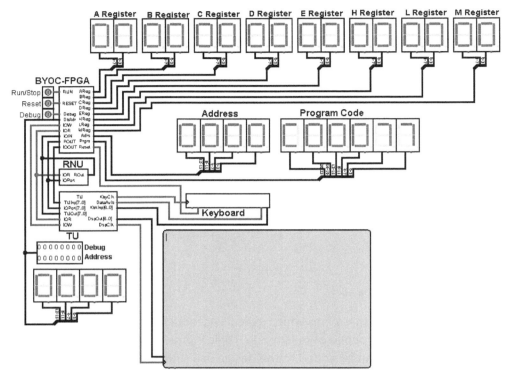

Across the top are the BYOC-24's registers. Below that is the current program address and program code. To the left and below is a debugging circuit. See Appendix F. And finally, the simulated keyboard and display.

This version of Logisim BYOC-24 CPU has the High/Low Guessing Game preloaded in its Program and Data ROMs.

To launch the game, follow these steps.

1. Click on the "pointy finger" in the upper left corner. When activated, you can toggle an input value by hovering the cursor over it and left clicking. Try it by changing the Debug input to "1". This activates the debug feature that halts execution at the Debug Address. Click again to reset Debug to "0" and turn debugging off.

2. Toggle the Reset input from "0" to "1" and back to "0". This prepares the CPU to begin execution at address 0x0000, the entry point for the game.

3. Toggle the Run input to "1" and the game title and instructions should print.

Note: If nothing happens, it's quite possible the Logisim clock is toggled off. While holding down the control key, press the "K" key once.

4. To use the keyboard, place the "pointy finger" cursor within the keyboard rectangle and left click. A faint blue oval should appear indicating the key board is active. Leaving the cursor there, begin typing and see the keys pressed echo on the display.

At this point, you should see what you type reappear on the display. You may notice that printing is slow compared to what you would see with a real computer because Logisim is a simulator running much slower.

Below is the user/computer dialog for a sample game.

```
Number Guessing Game

I am thinking of a number
between 1 and 100.
Press any key to continue
Your guess? 50
Too high.  Try again.
Your guess? 40
Too low.  Try again.
Your guess? 45
You got it in 3 tries.

I am thinking of a number
between 1 and 100.
Press any key to continue
```

In the next chapter, we prepare to develop assembly code for Tiny BASIC by first outlining a language specification.

Chapter 4
Tiny BASIC Specification

Our next step is to specify the Tiny BASIC language by describing its commands, statements and operational features.

Definitions:

Items enclosed in braces { …} are optional.

expr – A Tiny BASIC expression is a combination of one or more constants, variables, and the operators below.
- negation
+ addition
- subtraction
* multiplication
/ division – result (quotient) truncated to a whole number (remainder ignored)
% modulo – remainder after division

The order of operations is as follows:
negation
multiplication, division
addition, subtraction

The order of operation can be modified using parentheses as grouping symbols. Example: For 2*(A+1), variable A and constant 1 are grouped together by the parentheses and therefore added <u>before</u> multiplying by 2.

var - The letters A to Z represent integer variables with a value -32,768 to +32767 .

relop – Relational operators including < (less than), > (greater than), = (equal), and <> (not equal).

line_num – Tiny BASIC program line numbers ranging from 1 to 65535.

num – A number from 0 to 255.

Tiny BASIC Commands

1. **NEW** – Removes previous program so that a new Tiny BASIC program can be entered.

2. **RUN** – Executes the Tiny BASIC program.

3. **LIST** – Lists the Tiny BASIC program.

4. **LOAD num** – Loads Tiny BASIC program number "num" (beginning with 0) from the Data ROM.

Tiny BASIC Statements

1. **{LET} var=expr** – Assigns the computed value of expr to a numeric variable, var. Example: LET A=8; B=2*(A+1)

2. **INPUT var** – Accepts numeric input from the keyboard and stores it in a numeric variable var. Example: INPUT C

3. **PRINT {list}** – Outputs a list of text messages and/or evaluated expressions to the display device then skips to the next line. Text messages are enclosed in quotation marks. List items are separated by either a semicolon producing a single space or a comma producing a tab spacing of width 8. If PRINT ends with a semicolon or comma, no new line follows the indicated spacing. Example: PRINT "A=";2*V or PRINT "Time is";

4. **IF expr0 relop expr2 THEN line_num** – Compares two evaluated expressions and branches to the specified line number if true. "relop" is any one of the following combinations of relational operators: <, >, =, and <> (see below). Example: IF A<(B+C) THEN 20

5. **GOTO line_num** – Branches to a specified line number.

6. **GOSUB line_num** – Branches to a specified line number, which is the start of a Tiny BASIC subroutine.

7. **RETURN** –Returns from a Tiny BASIC subroutine to the instruction following the calling GOSUB.

8. **STOP** – When encountered, returns execution to the Editor/Command Mode.

9. **REM** – Skips to next program line. Used to add remarks to a program.

Operational Features

• **Editor/Command Mode** – After the Editor/Command Mode prompt ">", the user types a line of text terminated with ENTER key. Based on the text, one of the following happens:

If no line number followed by a command or statement:

Executes command/statement then returns to Editor/Command Mode.

If line number in range of 1 to 65535 followed by a statement:

If line number exists in program:

Existing line deleted, new line inserted, returns to Editor/Command Mode.

If line number does not exist:

New line inserted, then returns to Editor/Command Mode.

If line number only:

Existing line is deleted then returns to Editor/Command Mode

• **Execution mode** – After entering the RUN command, the Tiny BASIC program executes beginning at the first line.

Note: The terms "enter" and "entering" mean typing the given text and pressing the ENTER key.

• **Integer arithmetic** - Integer arithmetic is employed; values and calculations are limited to the range -32,768 to +32767.

• **Escape key** - The Escape key interrupts execution and LISTing a program. Control immediately returns to the Editor/Command Mode. Note: Logisim's keyboard simulator does not recognize the ESC key, so we use the backslash "\" key instead. Later, in the FPGA implementation, the PC keyboard uses the ESC key.

- **Not case sensitive** - Tiny BASIC is not case sensitive; i.e., let a=0 is the same as LET A=0.

If you are not familiar with program development with Tiny BASIC, Appendix G contains a brief synopsis.

In the next chapter, we use this language specification to lay out the Tiny BASIC design.

Chapter 5
Tiny BASIC Design

Tiny BASIC's design addresses flow, structure, and modularity. We start with "flow".

Tiny BASIC's Flow

Looking at Tiny BASIC's specification we see two distinct operating modes: (1) An editing and command execution mode and (2) a program execution mode. This suggests that Tiny BASIC flow should have two main loops, one responsible for an Editor/Command Mode and the other for an Execution Mode. The flow shown below is a "Modern Flow" modified to accommodate two main routines with a "RUN ⇆ STOP/ESC" provision for changing from one to the other.

Tiny BASIC Flow Chart

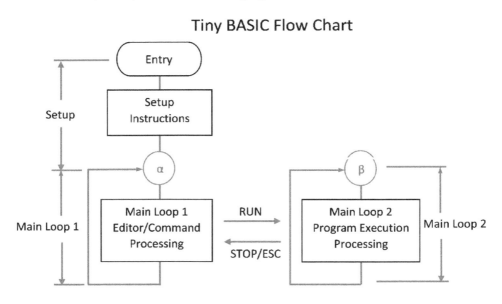

Tiny BASIC's Structure

Based on the dual main loop flow above, here is the Tiny BASIC functional flowchart

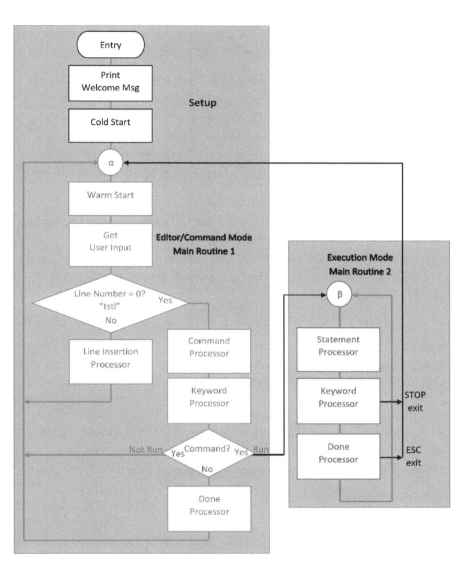

Contained within it are examples of sequence, selection, and repetition structure. The "Setup" code sequence executes only once at startup. Once finished, we enter "Main Loop 1" and "Main Loop 2", which are examples of repetition. In "Main Loop 1", we create and edit programs. In "Main Loop 2", we handle BASIC program execution.

Note: The functional flowchart has no overlapping loops. From this, we know that our eventual code will be free of confusing and error prone flow patterns.

In "Main Loop 1" (the Editor/Command Mode), we see examples of selection. A selection is made between lines with and without line numbers. Tiny BASIC program lines with a line number are added, changed, or deleted as per the Tiny BASIC specification. Program lines without a line number, are treated as a command or statement and immediately executed. Except for the RUN command, Tiny BASIC commands and statements return to the Editor/Command Mode after execution.

A second selection checks for the RUN command and, if found, transfers operation to "Main Loop 2" (the Execution Mode) where the program executes starting with the first line number. Though not shown explicitly, two additional selection points check for a STOP statement executed or the ESC key depressed. If either occurs, execution transfers back to "Main loop 1".

Tiny BASIC's Modularity

We take the same approach to modularity as we took when coding the High/Low Guessing Game assembly program; i.e., use a library of pre-coded subroutines that allows us to focus on the higher level and simpler to code parts of Tiny BASIC.

The first step is to study the Tiny BASIC functional flowchart above and identify predefined process blocks. Some of these are destined for the subroutine library and will be pre-coded for our convenience. Others will become routines and subroutines that we describe in detail. Below is the revised Tiny BASIC flowchart.

(Next page please)

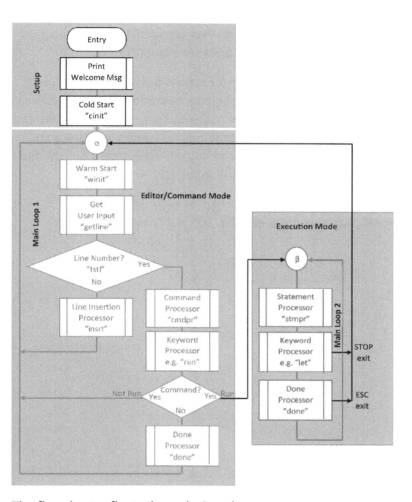

The flowchart reflects these design elements.

1. Tiny BASIC has a "Setup" prepares for a new program.
2. Tiny BASIC has two "Main Loops":
    a. "Main Loop 1" controlling program editing (the Editor/Command Mode)
    b. "Main Loop 2" controlling program execution (the Execution Mode)
3. RUN command, STOP statement, and pressing the ESC Key transfers execution between the main loops.

4. Tiny BASIC utilizes a mix of structural elements with no overlapping loops.

5 . For modularity, Tiny BASIC relies heavily on a library of subroutines.

Note: In general, predefine processes become subroutines or functions, but this is not always the case. As we will see, some code segments that perform specific tasks can be thought of as "modules" but not actually coded as subroutines. For example, the "Command Processor" predefined process block will ultimately become a code segment in "Main Loop 1", not a subroutine. The choice is often based on whether the task has utility beyond the specific application in the current program.

We are now ready to begin coding. In the next chapter, we begin with "Editor/Command Mode", which includes the "Setup" and "Main Loop 1" code segments.

Chapter 6
Editor/Command Mode

At startup, Tiny BASIC executes "Setup" and then "Main Loop 1". Let's first look at the "Setup" portion of the flowchart and the code that implements it.

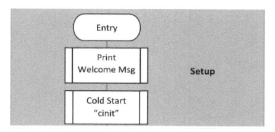

Setup Code

```
1 ──▶start: call     clrscr          ;Clear screen
2          lxi       irom,msg_wel    ;Print welcome message
           call      msgout
3          call      cinit           ;Cold start (new program)
           call      newline         ;Skip a line
```

1. The entry point "start" for Tiny BASIC is address 0x0000 in BYOC-24 CPU's Program ROM. To begin, we call Tiny BASIC library subroutine "clrscr" to clear the display screen. Specifications for this and all Tiny BASIC library subroutines can be found in Appendix D.

2. We call the "msgout" subroutine to print the welcome message "msg_wel" stored in Data ROM. As before, IROM points to the message.

3. We call the cold start initialization subroutine "cinit " to prepare Data RAM to accept a new program. As "Setup" code ends, we call "newline" to skip to the next line. When we call "getline" (see below), a second "newline" in effect skips a line before printing the Tiny BASIC prompt ">".

Below is the Main Loop 1 flowchart and editor/command processing code.

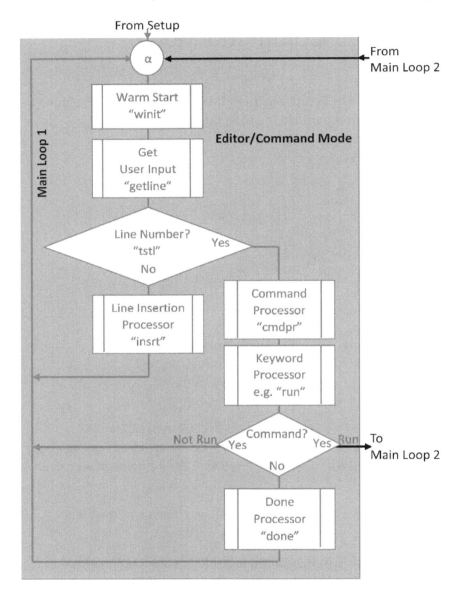

Main Loop 1 Code

```
1   wstart: call    winit           ;Warm start (keep current program)
            mvi     a,0b00000011    ;Reset push/pop & call/return stacks
            out     0xff,a
            call    newline         ;New line
2           call    getline         ;Get command or statement
            call    newline         ;New line
3           call    tstl            ;Command or program line
4           jnc     cmdpr           ;If a command, execute it
5           call    insrt           ;If a prgm line, insert/delete/replace
            jmp     wstart          ;Repeat
```

1. Label "wstart" is the entry point for "Main Loop 1". We call subroutine "winit" to perform any functions needed to prepare for a command or line insertion. For this version of Tiny BASIC, no processing is needed, so "winit" consists only of a RET instruction. Next, we include a code segment that resets the push/pop and call/return hardware stacks[v]. We take this precaution in case an error might have occurred leaving bytes on either or both stacks. We cannot include this code in "winit" because resetting the call/return stack while in a subroutine would cause a return error. Outputting a "1" to bits 0 and 1 of I/O port 0xff resets the stack address counter for the PP and CR Stacks, respectively.

2. Library subroutine "getline" gets a line of text from the user. In "getline", we print a "greater than" symbol ">"as prompt and then capture user keyboard input in Data RAM starting at address "bufstrt". When the user presses the "Enter" key, we store a CR byte as the end-of-line marker and return to Main Loop 1. We follow with a "newline" call to skip to the next line.

3. In "tstl" we perform these important tasks: (1) We determine the address where the keyword begins and store it in "txtstrt" and "txtstrt+1", LS byte first. We use this address later to locate the keyword at the beginning of a program line. (2) If the inputted line is preceded by line number, we convert the line number from ASCII to a 16-bit binary number and store it in "curlbl" and "curlbl+1", LS byte first. Lastly, we set the carry status bit then return. (2) If there is no line number, we prepare to

execute a command or statement by storing 0x0000 in "curlbl" and "curlbl+1" then reset the carry status bit and return.

4. Upon return from "tstl", a no-carry (status bit reset) indicates a command or statement is in the input buffer, so we branch to the command processor, "cmdpr".

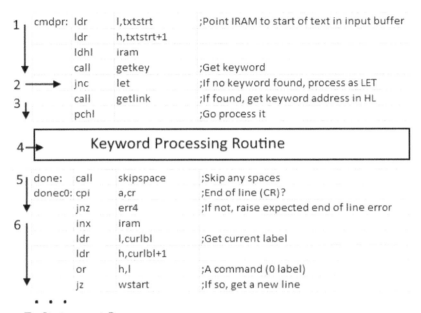

```
1   cmdpr:  ldr     l,txtstrt       ;Point IRAM to start of text in input buffer
            ldr     h,txtstrt+1
            ldhl    iram
            call    getkey          ;Get keyword
2           jnc     let             ;If no keyword found, process as LET
3           call    getlink         ;If found, get keyword address in HL
            pchl                    ;Go process it

4                   Keyword Processing Routine

5   done:   call    skipspace       ;Skip any spaces
    donec0: cpi     a,cr            ;End of line (CR)?
            jnz     err4            ;If not, raise expected end of line error
6           inx     iram
            ldr     l,curlbl        ;Get current label
            ldr     h,curlbl+1
            or      h,l             ;A command (0 label)
            jz      wstart          ;If so, get a new line
    . . .
```

To Statement Processor

1. We begin by loading IRAM with the address in "txtstrt" and "txtstrt+1" that points to the beginning of the keyword in the input buffer. Note that no BYOC-24 instruction directly loads IRAM with an address. Instead, we must first load HL with the address in "txtstrt" and "txtstrt+1" then load IRAM with HL using the "LDHL IRAM" instruction.

With IRAM pointing to the keyword, we call "getkey" to determine if the keyword is valid. If it is, "getkey" returns with carry status set and register C containing the numeric position of the keyword in the keyword link table "linktbl". If not found, "getkey" returns with the carry status reset.

Note: "getkey" does not distinguish between commands and statements. This follows the Tiny BASIC specification allowing statements as well as commands to be executed in Editor/Command Mode.

2. A "no carry" return from "getkey" means no command or statement was found. In keeping with the optional "LET" specification, we branch to the LET processing routine.

3. At this point, we call "getlink" to locate the address of the keyword's processing routine and return it in register pair HL. The "pchl" instruction jumps to the address in HL where the command or statement is processed.

4. For each command and statement keyword, there is a routine to process it. We describe them individually in later chapters.

Note: After processing, all commands except "RUN" terminate with a jump to warm start "wstart" then wait for user input. Statements, on the other hand, terminate with a jump to the "done" routine where code segments 5 and 6 below complete processing.

5. Entering the "done" routine, we first check to be sure that statement processing has ended on a CR. If not, the statement was incorrectly formed and we raise a syntax error.

6. Next, we point IRAM to the byte following CR and check for a 0x0000 in "curlbl" and "curlbl+1". Since we are processing a statement in Editor/Command Mode, the check is true, and we jump to warm start "wstart" and wait for user input.

Note: Again, in Editor/Command Mode, all processing except the RUN commands finally ends with a warm start and a wait for user input. If we had reached "done" while in Execution Mode, segment 6 would have sent us to process the statement in the next program line.

5. Reaching here, with the carry bit was set, means a line number was found at the beginning of the line, so we call the line insertion subroutine "insrt" to process it. The "insrt" subroutine is complex, as it must deal with these possible options including:

(1) If the new line consists of a line number only <u>and</u> a line with that line number exists, we delete the existing line then return.
(2) If the new line consists of a line number with a statement <u>and</u> an existing line with that number exists, we delete the existing line, insert the new line, then return.
(3) Otherwise, the new line is inserted then we return.

New lines are inserted in order by line number. In each case, "insrt" adjusts "prgend" to reflect changes to the program's length.

Here is the complete code for Main Loop 1.

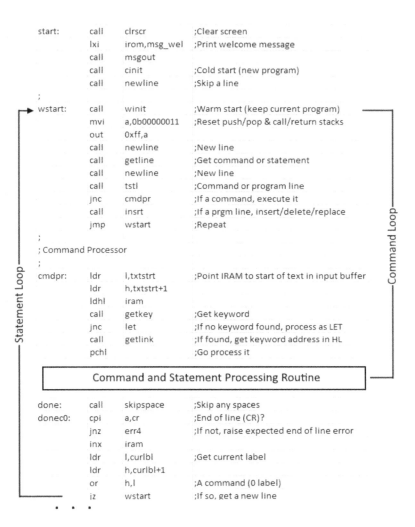

```
start:      call    clrscr          ;Clear screen
            lxi     irom,msg_wel    ;Print welcome message
            call    msgout
            call    cinit           ;Cold start (new program)
            call    newline         ;Skip a line
        ;
        wstart:  call    winit       ;Warm start (keep current program)
            mvi     a,0b00000011    ;Reset push/pop & call/return stacks
            out     0xff,a
            call    newline         ;New line
            call    getline         ;Get command or statement
            call    newline         ;New line
            call    tstl            ;Command or program line
            jnc     cmdpr           ;If a command, execute it
            call    insrt           ;If a prgm line, insert/delete/replace
            jmp     wstart          ;Repeat
        ;
        ; Command Processor
        ;
        cmdpr:  ldr     l,txtstrt    ;Point IRAM to start of text in input buffer
            ldr     h,txtstrt+1
            ldhl    iram
            call    getkey          ;Get keyword
            jnc     let             ;If no keyword found, process as LET
            call    getlink         ;If found, get keyword address in HL
            pchl                    ;Go process it
```

Command and Statement Processing Routine

```
done:     call    skipspace       ;Skip any spaces
donec0:   cpi     a,cr            ;End of line (CR)?
          jnz     err4            ;If not, raise expected end of line error
          inx     iram
          ldr     l,curlbl        ;Get current label
          ldr     h,curlbl+1
          or      h,l             ;A command (0 label)
          iz      wstart          ;If so, get a new line
              .   .   .
```

Statement Loop

Command Loop

Note: In keeping with our design criteria, the "Statement Loop" and "Command Loop" do not overlap. While it is not immediately obvious, no other loops within "Main Loop 1" overlap! I cannot emphasize enough how important this is to the avoidance of convoluted and error prone code.

In the next chapter, we examine Execution Mode.

Chapter 7
Execution Mode

To execute a Tiny BASIC program, we enter the "RUN" command changing execution from "Main Loop 1" to "Main Loop 2", the "Execution Mode".

Below is the "Main Loop 2" portion of Tiny BASIC flowchart followed by the execution mode processing code.

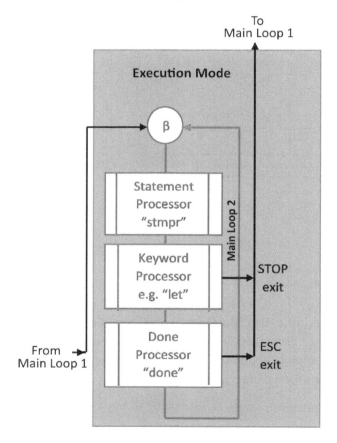

Main Loop 2 Code

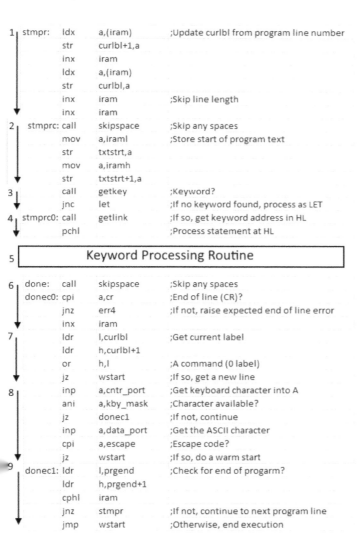

```
1  stmpr:   ldx    a,(iram)         ;Update curlbl from program line number
            str    curlbl+1,a
            inx    iram
            ldx    a,(iram)
            str    curlbl,a
            inx    iram             ;Skip line length
            inx    iram
2  stmprc: call    skipspace        ;Skip any spaces
            mov    a,iraml          ;Store start of program text
            str    txtstrt,a
            mov    a,iramh
            str    txtstrt+1,a
3           call   getkey           ;Keyword?
            jnc    let              ;If no keyword found, process as LET
4  stmprc0: call   getlink          ;If so, get keyword address in HL
            pchl                    ;Process statement at HL
```

5
Keyword Processing Routine

```
6  done:    call   skipspace        ;Skip any spaces
   donec0:  cpi    a,cr             ;End of line (CR)?
            jnz    err4             ;If not, raise expected end of line error
            inx    iram
7           ldr    l,curlbl         ;Get current label
            ldr    h,curlbl+1
            or     h,l              ;A command (0 label)
            jz     wstart           ;If so, get a new line
8           inp    a,cntr_port      ;Get keyboard character into A
            ani    a,kby_mask       ;Character available?
            jz     donec1           ;If not, continue
            inp    a,data_port      ;Get the ASCII character
            cpi    a,escape         ;Escape code?
            jz     wstart           ;If so, do a warm start
9  donec1:  ldr    l,prgend         ;Check for end of progarm?
            ldr    h,prgend+1
            cphl   iram
            jnz    stmpr            ;If not, continue to next program line
            jmp    wstart           ;Otherwise, end execution
```

1. Upon entry, IRAM points to the line number of the current program line. We store the two-byte line number in "curlbl" and "curlb+1l", MS byte first then increments IRAM twice more to skip the line length byte.

2. We skip spaces in the program line then store the address of the keyword starting byte in "txtstrt" and "txtstrt+1", LS byte first.

3. We call library subroutine "getkey" to check if the keyword is found in the "keyword table". If so, we return with the carry set and the C register with the numeric position of the address of the keyword's processing routine in the keyword link table. If the keyword isn't found, we return with the carry reset. In this case, we assume a LET statement and branch on no carry to the LET processing routine.

4. Reaching this point means a valid keyword has been found. We call "getlink" to load the address of the keyword processing routine into HL and use the "pchl" instruction to transfer execution to the keyword processing routine.

5. In future chapters, we describe the statement processing routines in detail. All statement processing routines terminate by jumping to "done".

6. The Tiny BASIC statement should be fully processed when entering "done". We check that IRAM is pointing to the CR byte and , if not, we raise an expected end-of-line error.

7. We check for 0x0000 in "curlbl" and "curlbl+1". Since we are in Execution Mode, the current line number is in "curlbl" and "curlblb+1" and we continue at code segment 8.

8. We check if the user has pressed ESC. If so, we terminate the program by branching to "wstart" and re-entering "Editor/Command Mode".

Note: Normally the escape character is ASCII ESC. Logisim's keyboard simulator doesn't recognize ESC, so we use the backspace character, ASCII "\" instead.

8. Lastly, we check to see if IRAM is pointing past the program's end. If so, we terminate the program by branching to warm start "wstart" to wait for user input. Otherwise, we branch to "stmpr" and process the next statement.

Note: We could have raised as error here forcing the user to end the program with a STOP statement. By choosing not to, we create a third way to exit a program.

To further our understanding of Execution Mode, let's look at an example program. First, this is how it looks when first entered.

```
10 LET A=0
20 PRINT A
30 LET A=A+1
40 GOTO 20
```

This is how the program first looks after program lines are inserted into memory.

Note: The single underline bytes are the binary line number; the double is the line length byte.

```
              "let"
              IRAM
              ↓
{0}{10}{{10} LET A=0{13}{0}{20}{10} PRINT A{13}{0}{30}{12} LET A=A+1{13}{0}{40}{10} GOTO 20{13}
 0  1    2   3-10    11 12 13  14   15-22  23 24 25  26    27-36   37 38 39 40   41-48  49  50
 ↑                                                                                          ↑
prgstrt ─────────────────────────────── Data RAM Address ───────────────────────────→ prgend
```

When we enter the RUN command, IRAM points to program start "prgstrt" in Data RAM. We execute "stmpr", the start of "Main Loop 2". We update "curlbl" and "curlbl+1" to 0 and 10, respectively.

```
   "getkey"→"getlink"
        IRAM
        ↓
{0}{10}{{10} LET A=0{13}{0}{20}{10} PRINT A{13}{0}{30}{12} LET A=A+1{13}{0}{40}{10} GOTO 20{13}
 0  1    2   3-10    11 12 13  14   15-22  23 24 25  26    27-36   37 38 39 40   41-48  49  50
 ↑                                                                                          ↑
prgstrt                                                                                 prgend
```

We skip the line length byte and point IRAM to the first byte of keyword LET. We call "getkey" and recognize LET as a keyword. We call "getlink" to get the address of the "let" processing routine.

```
              "let"
              IRAM
              ↓
{0}{10}{{10} LET A=0{13}{0}{20}{10} PRINT A{13}{0}{30}{12} LET A=A+1{13}{0}{40}{10} GOTO 20{13}
 0  1    2   3-10    11 12 13  14   15-22  23 24 25  26    27-36   37 38 39 40   41-48  49  50
 ↑                                                                                          ↑
prgstrt                                                                                 prgend
```

We jump to the LET processor and assign zero to variable A.

"done"
IRAM
⬇
{0}{10}{{10} LET A=0{13}{0}{20}{10} PRINT A{13}{0}{30}{12} LET A=A+1{13}{0}{40}{10} GOTO 20{13}

0 1   2   3-10   11 12 13 14   15-22 23 24 25 26   27-36   37 38 39 40   41-48 49 50
↑   ↑
prgstrt   prgend

IRAM now points to CR (ASCII code 13). In the "done" routine, we check for the CR and jump back to "stmpr.

"stmpr"
IRAM . . .
⬇
{0}{10}{{10} LET A=0{13}{0}{20}{10} PRINT A{13}{0}{30}{12} LET A=A+1{13}{0}{40}{10} GOTO 20{13}

0 1   2   3-10   11 12 13 14   15-22 23 24 25 26   27-36   37 38 39 40   41-48 49 50
↑   ↑
prgstrt   prgend

We are back at the beginning of "Main Loop 2" ready to process the next line. Processing continues along these same lines until we reach line 40. There, we encounter the GOTO statement.

"goto"
IRAM
⬇
{0}{10}{{10} LET A=0{13}{0}{20}{10} PRINT A{13}{0}{30}{12} LET A=A+1{13}{0}{40}{10} GOTO 20{13}

0 1   2   3-10   11 12 13 14   15-22 23 24 25 26   27-36   37 38 39 40   41-48 49 50
↑   ↑
prgstrt   prgend

The GOTO statement changes IRAM to point to the beginning of line 20 as shown.

"stmpr"
IRAM . . .
⬇
{0}{10}{{10} LET A=0{13}{0}{20}{10} PRINT A{13}{0}{30}{12} LET A=A+1{13}{0}{40}{10} GOTO 20{13}

0 1   2   3-10   11 12 13 14   15-22 23 24 25 26   27-36   37 38 39 40   41-48 49 50
↑   ↑
prgstrt   prgend We

are back to line 20 at the start of "Main Loop 2" and the program repeats lines 20 to 40 endlessly or until the user presses ESC.

This completes examination of how program lines execute in "Main Loop 1" and "Mail Loop 2". In the next chapter, we look at the code that processes commands and statements.

Chapter 8
Tiny BASIC Commands

We use NEW, LIST, RUN, and LOAD commands to create, edit, and execute Tiny BASIC programs. In this chapter we describe how these commands are coded.

Recall the command mode processing code below.

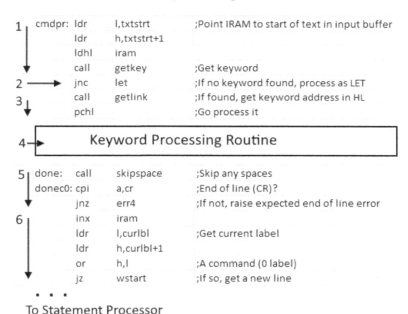

```
1   cmdpr: ldr     l,txtstrt       ;Point IRAM to start of text in input buffer
            ldr     h,txtstrt+1
            ldhl    iram
            call    getkey          ;Get keyword
2           jnc     let             ;If no keyword found, process as LET
            call    getlink         ;If found, get keyword address in HL
3           pchl                    ;Go process it

4           Keyword Processing Routine

5   done:   call    skipspace       ;Skip any spaces
    donec0: cpi     a,cr            ;End of line (CR)?
            jnz     err4            ;If not, raise expected end of line error
6           inx     iram
            ldr     l,curlbl        ;Get current label
            ldr     h,curlbl+1
            or      h,l             ;A command (0 label)
            jz      wstart          ;If so, get a new line
    . . .
    To Statement Processor
```

Section 4 is the keyword processing code associated with the command or statement being executed. Let's look at how we implement the simplest, NEW.

NEW Command

The NEW command calls the cold start initialization subroutine then jumps to "wstart", the entry point to "Main Loop 1". As previously described, "cinit" initializes a set of parameters that prepares Data RAM for a new program.

```
;
; NEW Processor
;
        new:  call    cinit           ;Do cold start
              jmp     wstart          ;Back to Main Loop 1
```

LIST Command

In a Tiny BASIC program line, the first two bytes are the 16-bit binary line number, MS byte first. The third byte is the line length. The remainder of the line is ASCII text. To print a program line, we must first convert the binary line number to ASCII text and print it. Next, we skip the line length byte and then print the remainder of the line as ASCII text.

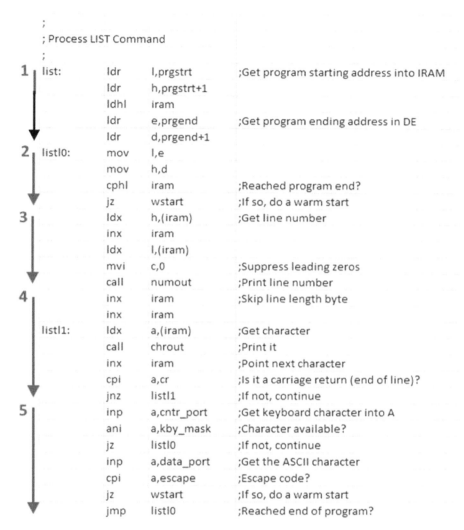

```
;
; Process LIST Command
;
1  list:       ldr     l,prgstrt       ;Get program starting address into IRAM
              ldr     h,prgstrt+1
              ldhl    iram
              ldr     e,prgend        ;Get program ending address in DE
              ldr     d,prgend+1
2  listl0:     mov     l,e
              mov     h,d
              cphl    iram            ;Reached program end?
              jz      wstart          ;If so, do a warm start
3             ldx     h,(iram)        ;Get line number
              inx     iram
              ldx     l,(iram)
              mvi     c,0             ;Suppress leading zeros
              call    numout          ;Print line number
4             inx     iram            ;Skip line length byte
              inx     iram
   listl1:     ldx     a,(iram)        ;Get character
              call    chrout          ;Print it
              inx     iram            ;Point next character
              cpi     a,cr            ;Is it a carriage return (end of line)?
              jnz     listl1          ;If not, continue
5             inp     a,cntr_port     ;Get keyboard character into A
              ani     a,kby_mask      ;Character available?
              jz      listl0          ;If not, continue
              inp     a,data_port     ;Get the ASCII character
              cpi     a,escape        ;Escape code?
              jz      wstart          ;If so, do a warm start
              jmp     listl0          ;Reached end of program?
```

1. Tiny BASIC programs start at Data RAM address "prgstrt" and ends at "prgend". We use IRAM to scan and print the Tiny BASIC program line, so we load index register IRAM with "prgstrt". We then load DE with "prgend" to check for the last line to print.

2. By comparing IRAM with DE, we check if the last program line has been printed. To use the "CPHL IRAM" instruction, we must preload HL with DE. If IRAM is at the program end, we jump to warm start.

3. The first two bytes of the program line are the line number. In this code, we load these two bytes into HL, the first and MS byte into H. We call the "numout" subroutine to convert the 16-bit value to ASCII text and print it. Passing zero in the C register, suppresses leading zeros.

4. Next, we skip the line length byte and print the line's ASCII text in the "listl1" loop. Encountering a CR byte signals the line's end and we fall through the "JNZ" instruction.

5. We check if the user has pressed the Escape key to interrupt listing. If so, we warm boot. If not, we jump back to "listl0", check for program end and, if not yet reached, print the next line.

RUN Command

The RUN command starts execution of a Tiny BASIC program by pointing IRAM to program start "prgstrt" and jumping to the "Main Loop 2" entry point "stmpr".

```
;
; RUN Processor
;
run:        ldr     l,prgstrt       ;Point IRAM to program start address
            ldr     h,prgstrt+1
            ldhl    iram
            jmp     stmpr           ;To statement processor
```

LOAD Command

This version of Tiny BASIC provides no way to save and load programs. We incorporate the LOAD statement as a partial solution to this deficiency. The LOAD statement provides a way to store Tiny BASIC programs in the Data ROM so that they can be loaded and executed. The format is "LOAD pnum" where "pnum" is the number of the program in the Data ROM.

To "save" a program, we copy the program text into the assembly language source (shown below), assemble it, then copy the object code into the BYOC-24 Data ROM.

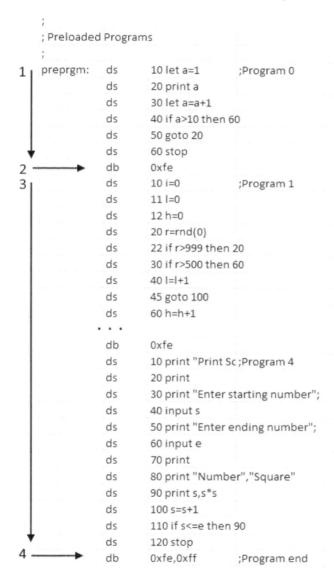

```
;
; Preloaded Programs
;
preprgm:    ds      10 let a=1          ;Program 0
            ds      20 print a
            ds      30 let a=a+1
            ds      40 if a>10 then 60
            ds      50 goto 20
            ds      60 stop
            db      0xfe
            ds      10 i=0              ;Program 1
            ds      11 l=0
            ds      12 h=0
            ds      20 r=rnd(0)
            ds      22 if r>999 then 20
            ds      30 if r>500 then 60
            ds      40 l=l+1
            ds      45 goto 100
            ds      60 h=h+1
            . . .
            db      0xfe
            ds      10 print "Print Sc ;Program 4
            ds      20 print
            ds      30 print "Enter starting number";
            ds      40 input s
            ds      50 print "Enter ending number";
            ds      60 input e
            ds      70 print
            ds      80 print "Number","Square"
            ds      90 print s,s*s
            ds      100 s=s+1
            ds      110 if s<=e then 90
            ds      120 stop
            db      0xfe,0xff          ;Program end
```

1. Beginning at "preprgm:", we copy and paste the first program ("pnum" = 0) into the third column. We then place "ds" (define string) in the second column of each program line.

2. Mark the end of a program with a "db" (define byte) in the second column and "0xFE" in the third column.

3. Following the same procedure, add other programs with a 0xFE byte following each one.

6. Place a 0xFE and 0xFF byte after the last program.

Provided there is space in the Data ROM, up to 256 programs can be stored and loaded with the LOAD command.

Here is the LOAD code.

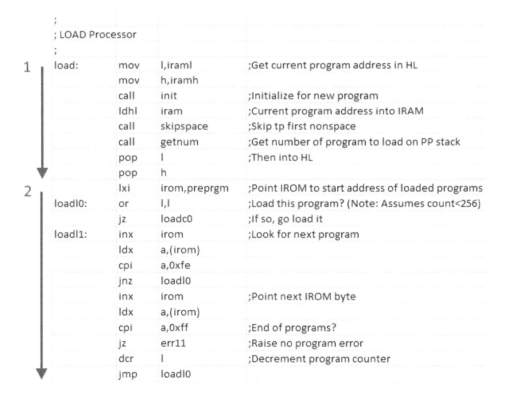

```
;
; LOAD Processor
;
1   load:       mov    l,iraml           ;Get current program address in HL
                mov    h,iramh
                call   init              ;Initialize for new program
                ldhl   iram              ;Current program address into IRAM
                call   skipspace         ;Skip tp first nonspace
                call   getnum            ;Get number of program to load on PP stack
                pop    l                 ;Then into HL
                pop    h
2               lxi    irom,preprgm      ;Point IROM to start address of loaded programs
    loadl0:     or     l,l               ;Load this program? (Note: Assumes count<256)
                jz     loadc0            ;If so, go load it
    loadl1:     inx    irom              ;Look for next program
                ldx    a,(irom)
                cpi    a,0xfe
                jnz    loadl0
                inx    irom              ;Point next IROM byte
                ldx    a,(irom)
                cpi    a,0xff            ;End of programs?
                jz     err11             ;Raise no program error
                dcr    l                 ;Decrement program counter
                jmp    loadl0
```

1. We call the cold start initialization subroutine to prepare for the new program. Next we load the program number into HL. (H is later ignored, so the number of possible programs is 256; that is, L can equal 0 to 255.) Lastly. we point IROM to the address "preprgm", the start of saved Tiny BASIC programs in the Data ROM. We use IROM to scan the saved programs in search of the one to load.

2. We search for the Tiny BASIC program that corresponds with the program number in register L. So long as L is greater than zero, we skip ahead to the next program in Data ROM and decrement L. When L reaches zero, we jump ahead to begin inputting the program. If we reach the 0xFF byte before L reaches zero, no program exists for that "pnum", and we raise an error.

```
3   loadc0:    mvi    l,lo(bufstrt)    ;Point HL to program start address
                mvi    h,hi(bufstrt)
    loadl2:    ldx    a,(irom)         ;Get program to load character
                or     a,a              ;End of line?
                jz     loadc1           ;If so, continue
                mov    m,a              ;Store it in input buffer
                adi    l,1              ;Point to next byte
                aci    h,0
                inx    irom
                jmp    loadl2           ;Repeat
4   loadc1:    mvi    m,cr             ;Place carriage return at end of line
                call   tstl             ;Command or statement (to insert)
                jnc    cmdpr            ;If a command, go execute it
                call   insrt            ;Insert the line
                inx    irom
                ldx    a,(irom)
                cpi    a,0xfe           ;End of program?
                jz     wstart           ;If so, do a warm start
                jmp    loadc0           ;Repeat
```

3 and 4. The remaining code copies each line of Data ROM program to the input buffer and handles insertion as if input had come from the keyboard. The end of the Tiny BASIC program is detected by finding the 0xFE byte, in which case, the code exits to warm start. The program is ready to run.

Note: "DS" places a 0x00 byte at the end of each program line while Tiny BASIC expects a CR. The code at the beginning of code segment 4 makes this substitution.

69

In the next chapter we begin our look at statement processing beginning with LET.

Chapter 9
LET Statement

The heart of the LET statement is the "expr" library subroutine that evaluates Tiny BASIC expressions. Not only is used with the LET statement, it plays an integral role in other statements and functions such as IF, GOTO, GOSUB, and the RND function.

Until now, we haven't described how library subroutines work. "expr" is a special case because it incorporates several important programming techniques.

Expression Subroutine

Tiny BASIC expressions consist of combinations variables (A to Z), constants (-32,768 to +32,767), operators (negation, addition "+", subtraction "-", multiplication "*", division "/", and modulo "%") and parentheses "(…)" as grouping symbols. Expressions follow the standard order of operations:

1. Parentheses (Highest Level)
2. Negation
3. Multiplication, division, modulo
4. Addition, subtraction (Lowest Level)

When more than two operations of the same order occur together, operations proceed from left to right.

For example, 2*(A-10/B) when A is 8 and B is 2 evaluates to 6. The quantity in the parentheses is evaluated first giving 3, then multiplied by 2 for the final value 6.

Consider this example: 40/10*2. The expression evaluates to either 8 or 2 depending on the order the operations are taken. "expr" evaluates operations from left to right giving 8 as the answer.

"expr" uses stack operations to manage data used in expression evaluation. By way of illustration, let's use a "stack" of index cards to evaluate the sum of three numbers 3, 8, and 4. To begin, write each number on an index card. Stack the cards in the order they are encountered above; i.e., 3 on the bottom, then 8, and 4 on top. Now, take the top two cards (4 and 8) off the stack and add them getting 12. Make a new card with 12 written on it and put it on top of the stack. The stack has the "12" card on top and the "3" card on bottom. Again, add the top two cards again getting 15. Write 15 on a card and put it on the stack. Drawing the top (and only) card on the stack we have the result, 15.

From the human point of view, this may seem a roundabout way of summing numbers, but it fits nicely into the way computers works. Using a stack, we don't have to worry with registers or locations in memory to store data values. All values reside on the stack and, after all operations have been performed, the result is also on the stack, ready to be accessed.

Another important advantage of using stack-based operations is that the "expr" subroutine is *recursive*. By that, we mean that the "expr" can call itself! Take this example 2+3*(A+8). Visualize the whole expression as EXPR0 and the part within the parentheses as a separate expression, EXPR1. We see later that we first call the "expr" subroutine to evaluate EXPR0. When we encounter the open parentheses, we call "expr" again and evaluate EXPR1 independently. The EXPR1 result ends up on the stack and becomes just another value used in evaluating EXPR0. Recursively calling "expr" is possible because all values are handled independently on the stack.

Should you want to know more about this way of handling expression evaluation, start by looking at the difference between *infix* notation and *Polish* notation. See https://en.wikipedia.org/wiki/Polish_notation.

The "expr" stack we use is the BYOC-24 CPU's Push/Pop (PP) Stack, which can store up to 255 8-bit values. The "push" instruction puts a specified register on to the PP Stack and the "pop" instruction places the top of the PP Stack into the specified register. Since the "push" and "pop" instructions handle only 8 bits at a time, 16-bit stack values require two "push" and two "pop" instructions.

Note: When saving a 16-bit value, we always PUSH the MS byte first, then the LS byte. Of course, we POP in the reverse order, LS byte first and then the MS byte.

Before examining "expr" code in detail, let's look at a functional outline.

EXPR

  A. Call TERM

  B. If "+" (Addition), then

      1. Call TERM

      2. Call ADD

      3. Jump to B

  C. If "-" (Subtraction), then

      1. Call TERM

      2. Call ADD

      3. Jump to B

  D. Return (end of expression evaluation)

TERM: 1. Call FACTOR

      2. If "*" (Multiplication), then

         a. Call FACTOR

         b. Call MULT

         c. Jump to A.2

      3. If "/" (Division), then

         a. Call FACTOR

         b. Call DIV

         c. Jump to A.2

      4. Return

FACTOR: i. A constant? If so, then get it and return.

      ii. A variable? If so, then get it and return

      iii. A "(..)? If so, then Call EXPR and return

      iv. Raise invalid expression error

To see how "expr" works, let's evaluate the expression 2+3*(A+8) assuming A is 2. At each point, the term "Stack[..]" shows the values on the stack, the left-most value being on top.

Pointing to the first value "2", we call EXPR:

1. After calling TERM and then FACTOR, constant 2 is on the top of the stack. Stack [2]

2. Finding no "*" and "/" we return to B. Stack [2]

3. Finding a "+", we call TERM again. 3 is put on the stack. Stack [3,2]

4. This time in TERM we encounter a "*" and call FACTOR again. Stack [3,2]

5. We now find the parentheses and call EXPR again. [Stack [3,2]

6. Calling TERM and FACTOR places a value of A, which is 2, on the stack. Stack [2,3,2]

7. Again, calling TERM and FACTOR yields 8. Stack [8,2,3,2]

8. We are now at B.2 and call ADD, adding the top two value on the stack, 8+2, getting 10 and we exit the second call to EXPR. Stack [10,3,2]

9. At B.2.b, we multiply the two top values on the stack getting 30. Stack [30,2]

10. After a few more checks, we are at C.2 adding the remaining stack values for a final value of 32. Stack [32]

11. Exiting the first call of EXPR, the top of the stack is 32.

Again, this seems like a lot of time consuming steps, but it's no problem for a computer executing millions of instructions per second!

Let's now look at the code for "expr" that implements Tiny BASIC expressions. To begin, we look at the highest level code section, parts A, B, and C above.

(Next page please)

```
;
; TinyBASIC Math Package
;
expr:      ldx     a,(iram)      ;Get byte from Data RAM
           cpi     a,'+'         ;Is it a plus sign?
           jnz     exprc0        ;If not, continue
           inx     iram          ;If so, ignore it
           jmp     exprc1
exprc0:    ldx     a,(iram)      ;Get next byte from Data RAM
           cpi     a,'-'         ;Is it a negation?
           jnz     exprc1        ;If not, continue
           inx     iram          ;Point to next byte in Data RAM
           call    term          ;Evaluate a term
           call    neg           ;Negate the result
           jmp     exprc2        ;Continue
exprc1:    call    term
exprc2:    ldx     a,(iram)      ;Get byte from Data RAM
           cpi     a,'+'         ;Is it addition?
           jnz     exprc3        ;If not, continue
           inx     iram          ;Point next byte from Data RAM
           call    term          ;Get next term
           call    add           ;Add the two values
           jmp     exprc2        ;More additions/subtractions
exprc3:    ldx     a,(iram)      ;Get byte from Data RAM
           cpi     a,'-'         ;Is it subtraction?
           jnz     exprc4        ;If not, continue
           inx     iram          ;Point next byte from Data RAM
           call    term          ;Get next term
           call    sub           ;Subtract the two values
           jmp     exprc2        ;More additions/subtractions
exprc4:    ret                   ;Done with result on top of PP Stack
```

1. In case a "+" appears in front of a number or expression, we check and skip over it if found.

Note: In "expr", we do not call "skipspace" when scanning an expression. Instead, we use "LDX" that loads the scanned byte indirectly using IRAM as a pointer. While spaces improve readability, skipping them wastes processing time.   "Readability" refers to the ease with which a human reader can comprehend the purpose, flow, and function of the code.

2. A minus sign representing negation is also a possibility. In this case, we skip over the minus sign and call the "term" subroutine leaving the result on top of the stack. We then call the "neg" subroutine to negate the top of the stack. The "term" call is skipped because the first term value is now on top of the stack. We move on to check for addition (a "+" sign).

3. We call "term" to put the first term of the expression on the stack (if it's not already there) and check for a "+" sign indicating addition. If found, we call "term" again and call the "add" subroutine to add the two term values on the stack leaving the sum on stack. We jump back to check for another addition and/or subtraction.

4 & 5. If no "+'" sign was found in step 3, we check for a "-" sign indicating subtraction. The code is like step 3 except we call the "sub" routine that subtracts the second term value from the first term value leaving the difference on the stack. The code then jumps back to check for another addition and/or subtraction.

Now let's turn to the next code level, the "term" section.

```
        ;
 1    term:     call    factor      ;Get first factor
      exprc5:   ldx     a,(iram)    ;Get byte from Data RAM
                cpi     a,'*'       ;Is it multiplication?
                jnz     exprc6      ;If not, continue
 2              inx     iram        ;Point to next byte from Data RAM
                call    factor      ;Get second factor
                call    mul         ;Multiply them
                jmp     exprc5      ;More multiplications/divisions
        ;
 3    exprc6:   ldx     a,(iram)    ;Get byte from Data RAM
                cpi     a,'/'       ;Is it division?
                jnz     exprc7      ;If not, continue
 4              inx     iram        ;Point to next byte from Data RAM
                call    factor      ;Get second factor
                call    div
                jmp     exprc5      ;More multiplications/divisions
 5    exprc7:   ret
```

1. A term must contain at least one factor, so our first step is to call the "factor" subroutine. Upon return, a single result is on top of the stack. We then check for an

"*" indicating multiplication. If none is found, we continue to code segment 3 and check for a "/" indicating division.

2. Having found an "*", we skip over it and call "factor" again. The two values to be multiplied are now on the stack. We call the "mul" subroutine that multiplies the top two values leaving the result on top of the stack.

3. We check for a "/" indicating division. In none is found, we return with just the one factor on top of the stack.

4. Preparing for division, we get the second value on the stack and call the "div" subroutine to divide the first factor by the second (dividend by divisor).

5. Regardless of whether there was multiplication or division, we always return with one value on top of the stack.

Finally, we look at the lowest level, the "factor" code.

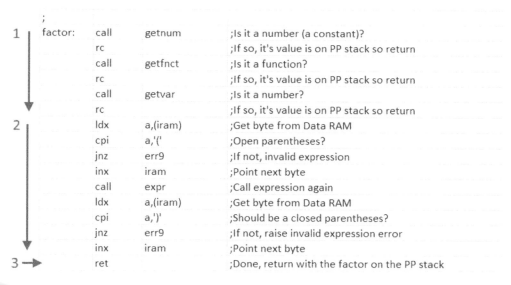

1. A Tiny BASIC factor must be one of four things: (1) a constant, (2) a variable, (3) a function, or (4) another expression enclosed in parentheses. Functions are essentially subroutines that take a parameter (only one for Tiny BASIC), operate on it in some way, and produce a single result that is returned on the top of the stack.

This version of Tiny BASIC has only one function, RND, that returns a pseudo-random number from 1 to 1000. It is useful in coding games or experimenting with random numbers. See Appendix E for more information.

The three subroutines ("getnum", "getfnct", and "getvar") function in the same way. Each looks to see if IRAM is pointing to a valid item of its type then places the associated value on the stack. A return with the carry status bit set means that the item was found. In such a case, we return with the factor value on top of the stack.

2. If we fail all three checks, the only possibility left is a "(" indicating a grouped expression. We check for an "(" and an "invalid expression" error is raised if not found. If one is found, we skip over the "(" and call "expr" again.

Note: We can call "expr" from within "expr" as many times as we encounter open parentheses, limited only by the size of the stack. No matter how complicated an expression, we finally end up with a single value on the stack!

Below is an example with a rather complicated expression handled easily with the "expr" subroutine.

```
>list

10 a=10
20 b=2
30 c=3
40 d=-2*(16/b+3*a*(c+4*b/(c-b))+16)
50 print d

>run

-708
```

3. At this point, "expr" is finished, and the resulting value is on top of the stack. Execution returns to the calling routine where the value is popped off the stack and used.

Adding "expr" to the subroutine library means we can use it whenever we want to capture a Tint BASIC expression value!

78

LET Statement

Let's look now at the LET processor. The general format for the LET statement is "LET var=expr" where "var" is a variable A-Z and "expr" is a Tiny BASIC expression.

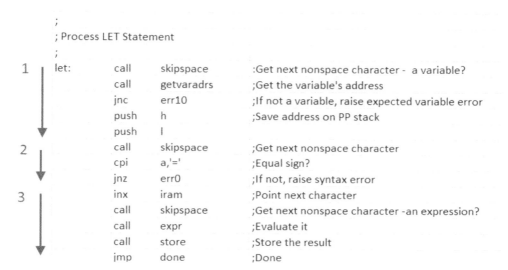

```
;
; Process LET Statement
;
let:      call    skipspace     :Get next nonspace character -  a variable?
          call    getvaradrs    ;Get the variable's address
          jnc     err10         ;If not a variable, raise expected variable error
          push    h             ;Save address on PP stack
          push    l
          call    skipspace     ;Get next nonspace character
          cpi     a,'='         ;Equal sign?
          jnz     err0          ;If not, raise syntax error
          inx     iram          ;Point next character
          call    skipspace     ;Get next nonspace character -an expression?
          call    expr          ;Evaluate it
          call    store         ;Store the result
          jmp     done          ;Done
```

1. Should there be a space after the LET text, we skip over it. IRAM points to the variable, a letter A to Z. The "getvaradrs" subroutine checks for a variable and if one is found, carry is set and HL returns with the variable's address. If no variable is found, "getvaradrs" returns with carry reset and we raise a variable expected error.

Note: We will use the "store" subroutine in code segment 3 below. It requires us to push the target variable address onto the stack then the value itself. At this point, HL contains the variable's address, so we push it onto the stack. The value to be stored is pushed onto the stack in code segment 3 below.

2. We check for the "=" and raise a syntax error if missing.

3. In case there's a space before the expression starts, we call "skipspace". IRAM should now be pointing at the beginning of the expression, so we call "expr". Upon return, the top two items on the stack are the evaluated result of the expression and the address where it is to be stored. We call the "store" subroutine and we are finished.

We return from "expr" pointing to first byte passed the end of the expression, which should be a CR byte. All that's left to do is jump to the "done" routine.

Note: The LET keyword is optional. If "getkey" in either main loop doesn't find a valid keyword at the beginning of a command or statement, we assume the LET keyword and jump to the LET processing routine. If it is a LET statement, we execute it. If not, then we raise an error.

In the next chapter, we describe the INPUT and PRINT statements that permits users to communicate with the BYOC-24 CPU.

Chapter 10
INPUT and PRINT Statements

Tiny BASIC programs communicate with the user via INPUT and PRINT statements. The format of the INPUT statement is "INPUT var" where "var" is the variable A to Z that receives the numeric value entered on the keyboard by the user.

Operationally, the INPUT statement prints a question mark "?" to prompt the user to enter a numeric value. After the value is entered, the value is stored in the given variable.

INPUT Statement

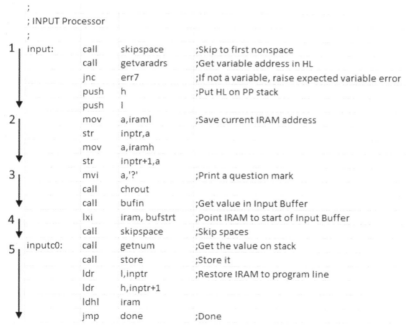

```
        ;
        ; INPUT Processor
        ;
1  input:    call    skipspace       ;Skip to first nonspace
             call    getvaradrs      ;Get variable address in HL
             jnc     err7            ;If not a variable, raise expected variable error
             push    h               ;Put HL on PP stack
             push    l
2            mov     a,iraml         ;Save current IRAM address
             str     inptr,a
             mov     a,iramh
             str     inptr+1,a
3            mvi     a,'?'           ;Print a question mark
             call    chrout
             call    bufin           ;Get value in Input Buffer
4            lxi     iram, bufstrt   ;Point IRAM to start of Input Buffer
             call    skipspace       ;Skip spaces
5  inputc0:  call    getnum          ;Get the value on stack
             call    store           ;Store it
             ldr     l,inptr         ;Restore IRAM to program line
             ldr     h,inptr+1
             ldhl    iram
             jmp     done            ;Done
```

1. Skipping spaces should put us at a variable (A to Z). We call "getvaradrs" to get its address. If no variable is found (carry reset), we raise an "expected variable

error". Otherwise (carry set), we fall through and save the variable address in HL on the PP Stack in preparation for using the "store" subroutine later.

2. In segment 3, we use library subroutine "bufin" to capture the user's inputted number. To use "getnum", IRAM must be pointing to the input buffer, but IRAM is in use scanning the Tiny BASIC program. Therefore, we must save IRAM in memory locations "inptr" and "inptr+1" before calling "getnum". Upon return, we restore IRAM.

3. We print the user prompt, a question mark "?", then call "bufin". Upon return, the inputted ASCII number is in the input buffer beginning at address "bufstrt".

4. We now switch IRAM to the start of the input buffer and skip any spaces.

5. We call "getnum" to convert the ASCII number at "bufstrt" to a 16-bit binary value on the PP Stack. We call "store" to store the number in the designated variable location. It only remains to reload IRAM with the previously saved address and jump to the "done" routine.

Note: The INPUT statement cannot be executed in Editor/Command Mode because the user's input would overwrite the INPUT statement creating an error condition.

PRINT Statement
PRINT statement logic is not simple. Stated in words it reads like this: "PRINT" prints expressions and/or string literals (text enclosed in quotation marks like "Hello World") with each separated by either (1) a semicolon ";" printing a single space between items or (2) a comma "," printing spaces to the next zone. "Zones" are eight character wide. Also, a semicolon or comma at the end of a PRINT statement suppresses a new line after single or zone spacing.

Before coding it, we capture the complex logic using a flowchart.

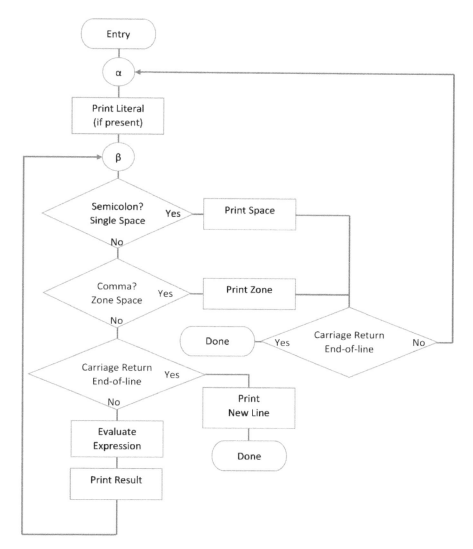

From the flowchart we create the PRINT processing code.

```
;
; Process PRINT Statement
;
```

<table>
<tr><td>1</td><td>print:</td><td>call</td><td>skipspace</td><td>;Get next nonspace character</td></tr>
<tr><td></td><td></td><td>call</td><td>printlit</td><td>;Print literal("..text..") if present</td></tr>
<tr><td>2</td><td>printc0:</td><td>call</td><td>skipspace</td><td>;Get next non-space character</td></tr>
<tr><td></td><td></td><td>cpi</td><td>a,';'</td><td>;Semicolon?</td></tr>
<tr><td></td><td></td><td>jnz</td><td>printc1</td><td>;If not, continue</td></tr>
<tr><td></td><td></td><td>mvi</td><td>a,' '</td><td>;Print space</td></tr>
<tr><td></td><td></td><td>call</td><td>chrout</td><td></td></tr>
<tr><td></td><td></td><td>inx</td><td>iram</td><td>;Point next program character</td></tr>
<tr><td></td><td>printe:</td><td>call</td><td>skipspace</td><td>;Get first non-space character</td></tr>
<tr><td></td><td></td><td>cpi</td><td>a,cr</td><td>;End of line?</td></tr>
<tr><td></td><td></td><td>jz</td><td>done</td><td>;If so, done w/o new line</td></tr>
<tr><td></td><td></td><td>jmp</td><td>print</td><td>;If not, back for more items to print</td></tr>
</table>

```
;
```

<table>
<tr><td>3</td><td>printc1:</td><td>cpi</td><td>a,','</td><td>;Zone Spacing?</td></tr>
<tr><td></td><td></td><td>jnz</td><td>printc2</td><td>;If not, continue</td></tr>
<tr><td></td><td></td><td>inx</td><td>iram</td><td>;Point next program character</td></tr>
<tr><td></td><td>printl0:</td><td>ldr</td><td>a,zone</td><td>;Get zone counter</td></tr>
<tr><td></td><td></td><td>ani</td><td>a,0b00000111</td><td>;Mask lower 3 bits</td></tr>
<tr><td></td><td></td><td>jz</td><td>printe</td><td>;If zero, done</td></tr>
<tr><td></td><td></td><td>mvi</td><td>a,' '</td><td>;Print a space</td></tr>
<tr><td></td><td></td><td>call</td><td>chrout</td><td></td></tr>
<tr><td></td><td></td><td>jmp</td><td>printl0</td><td>;Back to check if end of zone reached</td></tr>
</table>

```
;
```

<table>
<tr><td>4</td><td>printc2:</td><td>cpi</td><td>a,cr</td><td>;End of line?</td></tr>
<tr><td></td><td></td><td>jnz</td><td>printc3</td><td>;If not, continue</td></tr>
<tr><td></td><td></td><td>call</td><td>newline</td><td>;New line</td></tr>
<tr><td></td><td></td><td>jmp</td><td>done</td><td>;Done</td></tr>
</table>

```
;
```

<table>
<tr><td>5</td><td>printc3:</td><td>call</td><td>expr</td><td>;Assume an expression and evaluate it</td></tr>
<tr><td></td><td></td><td>call</td><td>printnum</td><td>;Print numeric result</td></tr>
<tr><td></td><td></td><td>jmp</td><td>printc0</td><td>;Check for end of line</td></tr>
</table>

1. Upon entry, we check for a literal ("…text…") and print it. The "printlit" subroutine assumes the literal begins and ends with a quotation mark printing the text in between.

2. We check for a semicolon and if present, print a single space. If followed by a carriage return, we immediately exit without skipping to the next line.

3. We check for a comma indicating a zone print. In this case, the number of spaces to print is determined this way. After each new line, we zero "zone" memory. Each time we print a character, we increment "zone". When a zone print is encountered, we print spaces until the last three bits of "zone" are zero indicating the end of a 8 character wide zone. This code represents a quick and easy approach that only works for a zone width of 8. For other widths, the code would be considerably more complex.

4. We arrive here after printing a literal or an expression and, if a CR is found, call "new line" to skip to the next line. We end PRINT by jumping to "done".

5. Having exhausted all other possibilities, we assume IRAM points to an expression and we call "expr". We then call "printnum" to print the number now on top of the PP Stack. From here, we jump back to the semicolon and comma checks. Doing so, we require either a semicolon or comma appear between literals and expressions.

Below is a short program demonstrating the INPUT and PRINT statements.

```
>list

10 print "Print Squares Demo"
20 print
30 print "Enter starting number";
40 input s
50 print "Enter ending number";
60 input e
70 print
80 print "Number","Square"
90 print s,s*s
100 s=s+1
110 if s<=e then 90
120 stop

>|
```

Executing it produces:

```
>run

Print Squares Demo

Enter starting number ?1
Enter ending number ?5

Number Square
1       1
2       4
3       9
4       16
5       25

STOP at line 120
```

While the output formatting options are limited, they do the job!

In the next chapter, we look at the GOTO and IF...THEN statements.

Chapter 11
GOTO and IF..THEN Statements

GOTO and IF...THEN statements provide unconditional and conditional branching in Tiny BASIC programs. As for code, GOTO and THEN are the same; the only difference being that THEN is conditioned on a numeric comparison in the IF portion of the IF...THEN statement.

GOTO Statement

Let's look at the GOTO statement first. The "GOTO line_num" transfers execution to the program line with line number "line_num". To find this program line, we use a simple linear search. Starting with the first program line, we check line numbers until the target line number is found. The obvious disadvantage of this approach is the increasing time required to find a line as the program size increases.

Early on, we addressed this disadvantage by preprocessing program lines before storing them in Data RAM. First, we converted the line number from ASCII to binary to reduce the time needed to compare line numbers. Second, we added a line length byte to speed movement from one line to the next. Taken together, these increase search speed to tolerable levels.

Note: Other methods were tried at various times in Tiny BASIC's history, but the improvements were never sufficiently better to warrant changing from a linear search. For programs of the size generally created for Tiny BASIC, the processing overhead in these more advanced search algorithms cancelled any search speed advantage.

Library subroutine "fndlbl" performs the linear line number search.

(Next page please)

```
;
; Get Start of Line Matching Label DE into HL  (Carry set if found)
;
```

1	fndlbl:	ldr	l,prgstrt	;Get start of program in HL
		ldr	h,prgstrt+1	
		ldr	c,prgend	;Get end of program in BC
		ldr	b,prgend+1	
2	fndlbll:	cmp	h,b	;Reached end of program?
		jnz	fndlblc0	
		cmp	l,c	
		rz		;If so, return carry reset
3	fndlblc0:	cmp	m,d	;MS Byte match?
		jnz	fndlblc1	;If not, skip to next line
		adi	l,1	;Point LS Byte
		aci	h,0	
		cmp	m,e	;LSB match?
		jnz	fndlblc2	;If not, skip to next line
		sui	l,1	;Fount it!
		sbi	h,0	;Point back to start of line
		stc		;Set carry
		ret		;Return
4	fndlblc1:	adi	l,1	;Point next byte (LSB)
		aci	h,0	
	fndlblc2:	adi	l,1	;Point next byte (line length)
		aci	h,0	
		mov	a,m	;Get length of line in A
		add	l,a	;Compute new line start
		aci	h,0	
		jmp	fndlbll	;Try again

1. We enter the subroutine with target "line number" in register pair DE. We set up register pair HL to scan program memory beginning at "prgstrt".   Register BC is loaded with the program end address "prgend", so we know when to end the search.

2. If program end is reached, we return with the carry reset indicating the line number was not found.

3. We compare the current line number pointed to by HL with the target "line number" in DE. If found, we return with carry set and HL pointing to the beginning of the target program line.

4. If there is a mismatch, we point to the beginning of the next program line by simply adding the line length to the current address in HL.

Using "fndlbl", GOTO processing code is straightforward.

```
        ;
        ; GOTO Processor
        ;
1   goto:     call    skipspace    ;Get line target line number on PP stack
              call    expr
              pop     e            Load it into DE
              pop     d
2             call    fndlbl       ;Find the target line number
              jnc     err6         ;On carry reset, raise unknown line number er
              ldhl    iram         ;Point IRAM to new line
              jmp     stmpr        ;Go process it
```

1. After skipping spaces, we call "expr" to get the target line number.

Note: The target can be either a constant or a Tiny BASIC expression. Providing this "computed GOTO" capability is a powerful capability in the hands of a skilled programmer.

2. We pop the target line number now on the PP Stack into DE then call "fndlbl". Depending on the search result, we either raise an error (carry reset) or jump to the statement processor "stmpr" (carry set) to continue execution at the new line number.

F Statement

The IF...Then statement looks like this "IF expr0 relop expr2 THEN line-num" where "expr0" and "expr1" are numeric expressions; "relop" is a relational operator (see below); and "line num" is the line number of the program line to which we transfer if the relational expression is true. If false, execution continues at the next program line.

The allowed relational operators are as follows:

Less than "<"
Greater than ">"
Less than equal to "<="
Greater than equal to ">="
Equal to "="
Not equal to "<>"

The coding difficulty here is finding a simple way to handle all these options. Our choice is to create a "relop" status byte and assign bits to indicate which relational operators are specified in the given IF...THEN statement. The "relop" status byte also keeps track of how many operators have been chosen, the maximum being two. Here's how it works.

1. We call "expr" to get "expr0" on the PP Stack.

2. The status byte is first set to 0b10000000. Bit 7 is the "pass number" bit. It is "1" on the first pass and "0" on the second pass. After the second pass, there should be no more relational operators.

The other bits are assigned based on "relop" as follows:

Bit 0 Set to "1" if the pass encountered a less than "<".
Bit 1 Set to "1" If the pass encountered a greater than ">".
Bit 2 Set to "1" if the pass encountered an "=".

2. After the two passes, "relop" status bit 7 is "0" and bits 0 to 2 are set or reset according to the "relop" operators encountered.

3. We call "expr" a second time to get "expr1" on the PP Stack.

4. We call the "sub" subroutine to subtract "expr1" from "expr0".

5. If the result is zero indicating that expr0 = expr1 and the "=" status bit 2 is set, we process the THEN statement and transfer execution to the "THEN" line number. Otherwise, we skip the text following THEN and look for the CR byte. When found, we jump to "done".

6. If the result is negative indicating expr0 < expr1 and the "<" status bit 0 is set, we process the THEN statement and transfer execution to the "THEN" line number. Otherwise, we skip the text following THEN section and look for the CR byte. When found, we jump to "done".

7. If the result is positive indicating expr0 > expr1 and the ">" status bit 1 is set, we process the THEN statement and transfer execution to the target line number. Otherwise, we skip the text following THEN section and look for the CR byte. When found, we jump to "done".

This logic is easy to code though a bit lengthy. Let's look at it in two parts. Here is Part 1.

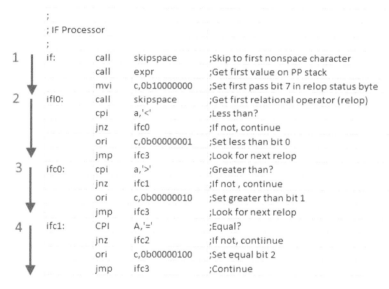

```
        ;
        ; IF Processor
        ;
1   if:         call    skipspace       ;Skip to first nonspace character
                call    expr            ;Get first value on PP stack
                mvi     c,0b10000000    ;Set first pass bit 7 in relop status byte
2   ifl0:       call    skipspace       ;Get first relational operator (relop)
                cpi     a,'<'           ;Less than?
                jnz     ifc0            ;If not, continue
                ori     c,0b00000001    ;Set less than bit 0
                jmp     ifc3            ;Look for next relop
3   ifc0:       cpi     a,'>'           ;Greater than?
                jnz     ifc1            ;If not , continue
                ori     c,0b00000010    ;Set greater than bit 1
                jmp     ifc3            ;Look for next relop
4   ifc1:       CPI     A,'='           ;Equal?
                jnz     ifc2            ;If not, contiinue
                ori     c,0b00000100    ;Set equal bit 2
                jmp     ifc3            ;Continue
```

1. We call "expr" to get the first value "expr0". We load the C register with the initial value of the "relop" status bit. Bit 7 is set indicating we are making the first pass to collect relational operators.

2. We check for less than "<", set bit 0 of C if found, and prepare for a second pass at "ifc3".

3. We check for greater than ">", set bit 1 of C if found, and prepare for a second pass at "ifc3".

4. We check for an equal sign "=", set bit 2 of C if found, and prepare for a second pass at "ifc3".

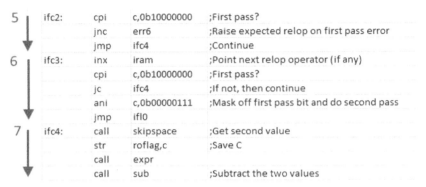

```
5    ifc2:    cpi    c,0b10000000    ;First pass?
              jnc    err6            ;Raise expected relop on first pass error
              jmp    ifc4            ;Continue
6    ifc3:    inx    iram            ;Point next relop operator (if any)
              cpi    c,0b10000000    ;First pass?
              jc     ifc4            ;If not, then continue
              ani    c,0b00000111    ;Mask off first pass bit and do second pass
              jmp    if10
7    ifc4:    call   skipspace       ;Get second value
              str    roflag,c        ;Save C
              call   expr
              call   sub             ;Subtract the two values
```

5. If we reach here on the first pass and no relational operator is found, then we raise a missing relational operator error.

6. We prepare for the second pass in case there are two relational operators.

7. When we reach here, C contains the completed "relop" status byte, which we store in memory location "roflag". We can't leave it in C because we are about to call "expr" that uses C. We call "expr" a second time to get the value "expr1" and then call "sub" to subtract "expr1" from "expr0".

The top of the PP Stack has the difference value and we are ready for part 2 of the code.

```
1    pop    l              ;Result 0?
     pop    h
2    ldr    c,roflag       ;Restore C
     mov    a,h
     or     a,l
     jnz    ifc5           ;If not, continue
     mov    a,c            ;Equal bit set?
     ani    a,0b00000100
     jnz    stmprc         ;If so, process THEN
     jmp    ifdone         ;If not, then done
```

1. The difference of "expr0" and "expr1" is on the PP Stack. We pop this value into HL.

2. After restoring the "relop" status byte into the C register, we check if the difference is zero indicating the two values are equal. To check if HL is zero, we move H to A and OR A with L. ORing H directly with L would change H and make further HL checks invalid. You must always avoid traps like this, as they cause untold debugging misery!

If HL is zero, we check if the equal status bit is set using an AND immediate 0x04 (the "=" bit "1") to check if the corresponding bit in C is "1". If not zero, the "equal" check is "true", and we process the THEN (the same as GOTO) transferring execution to the target line number. If not, the "equal" result is "false", and we skip the remainder of the line looking for the CR character. We jump to "done"

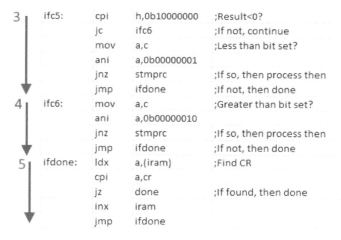

```
3   ifc5:     cpi    h,0b10000000    ;Result<0?
              jc     ifc6            ;If not, continue
              mov    a,c             ;Less than bit set?
              ani    a,0b00000001
              jnz    stmprc          ;If so, then process then
              jmp    ifdone          ;If not, then done
4   ifc6:     mov    a,c             ;Greater than bit set?
              ani    a,0b00000010
              jnz    stmprc          ;If so, then process then
              jmp    ifdone          ;If not, then done
5   ifdone:   ldx    a,(iram)        ;Find CR
              cpi    a,cr
              jz     done            ;If found, then done
              inx    iram
              jmp    ifdone
```

3. This code segment performs a similar check for "less than", looking for a negative difference of "expr0" and "expr1".

4. We arrive here if the difference is positive and check if the "greater than" bit is set. The result is handled the same as 2 and 3.

5. This last section ("ifdone" code) is used with "false" results, in which case, we skip the THEN portion of the IF...THEN and execute the next statement.

In the next chapter, we describe the code for GOSUB/RETURN, and REM statements.

Chapter 12 – GOSUB/RETURN, STOP, and REM Statements

GOSUB and RET (Return) Statements

"GOSUB line num" is like "GOTO line num" in that it transfers execution to the program line with line number "line_num"". The only difference is that we save a return address on the PP Stack. Later, when a RET instruction executes, we pop the return address off the PP Stack, look for the end of the GOSUB line, and jump to "done". Execution continues at the line following the GOSUB. Thus, we have added subroutines to Tiny BASIC's toolbox. With this approach, calling a subroutine within a subroutine is permissible up to the limit of PP Stack size!

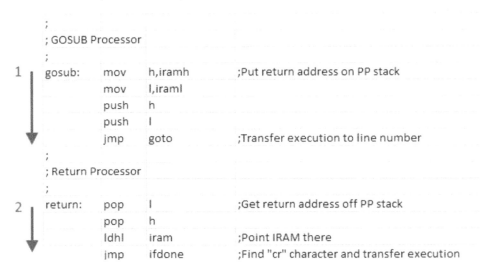

```
        ;
        ; GOSUB Processor
        ;
1   gosub:    mov    h,iramh        ;Put return address on PP stack
              mov    l,iraml
              push   h
              push   l
              jmp    goto           ;Transfer execution to line number
        ;
        ; Return Processor
        ;
2   return:   pop    l              ;Get return address off PP stack
              pop    h
              ldhl   iram           ;Point IRAM there
              jmp    ifdone         ;Find "cr" character and transfer execution
```

1. We save the current program address on the PP Stack and jump to "goto".

Note: Though it may seem problematic to use the PP Stack for arithmetic calculations and for return addresses, there is no conflict. After processing a statement, no arithmetic results are left on the PP Stack to conflict with return addresses.

94

2. Upon return, we simply pop the return address off the PP Stack and use the "ifdone" routine to find the end of line CR, jump to "done" and continue execution at the next program line.

STOP Statement

We use the STOP statement to exit the Execution Mode and return to the Editor/Command Mode. We simply jump to warm start "wstart" and we're back in the Command/Editor Loop!

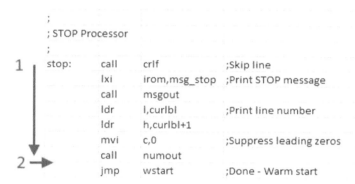

```
;
; STOP Processor
;
stop:    call    crlf                        ;Skip line
         lxi     irom,msg_stop ;Print STOP message
         call    msgout
         ldr     l,curlbl                    ;Print line number
         ldr     h,curlbl+1
         mvi     c,0                         ;Suppress leading zeros
         call    numout
         jmp     wstart                      ;Done - Warm start
```

1. Before warm starting, we print a STOP message. The STOP line number is in "curlbl", which we load in HL and print with "numout". We zero the C register to suppress leading zeroes.

2. We jump to warm start and enter the Editor/Command Mode.

REM Statement

The REM (remark) statement skips to the next statement essentially doing nothing.

```
;
; REM Processor
;
rem:     ldr     l,txtstrt           ;Get start of text in IRAM
         ldr     h,txtstrt+1
         ldhl    iram
         jmp     ifdone              ;Look for CR then Done
```

1. We load IRAM with the start of text address then jump to "ifdone". There we look for the CR byte and jump to done.

With the REM statement, we have covered all Tiny BASIC statements and commands. Next, we look at how to use Logisim to test Tiny BASIC and put it through its paces.

Chapter 13
Testing Tiny BASIC

In Chapter 3, we introduced Logisim and showed how to use it to test the assembly version of the High/Low Guessing Game. In this chapter, we do the same with Tiny BASIC. Follow the instructions below to load Logisim files "tb-l-prom.txt" and "tb-l-drom.txt" into the Logisim Program ROM and Data ROM, respectively.

To load Logisim Program ROM:
    From Navigation Pane, right-click "BYOC-I" and click "Edit Circuit Layout"
        Right-click "Program ROM" and click "Load Image…"
        Navigate to "tb-l-prom.txt" and click OK.

To load Logisim Data ROM
    From Navigation Pane, right-click "BYOC-I" and click "Edit Circuit Layout"
        Right-click "Data ROM" and click "Load Image…"
        Navigate to "tb-l-drom.txt" and click OK.

Reset and Run the BYOC-24 CPU. The title message should print as below.

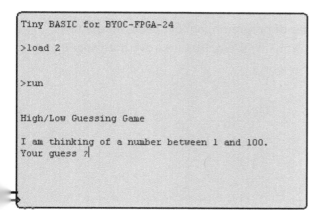

```
Tiny BASIC for BYOC-FPGA-24

>load 2

>run

High/Low Guessing Game

I am thinking of a number between 1 and 100.
Your guess ?
```

Enter "load 2" to load the Tiny BASIC version of the High/Low Guessing Game. Enter "list" to list it.

```
10 print
15 print "High/Low Guessing Game"
20 print
25 print "I am thinking of a number between 1 and 100."
30 gosub 100
35 t=0
40 let t=t+1
45 print "Your guess";
50 input g
55 if g<>r then 70
60 print "You got it in ";t;"tries"
65 goto 10
70 t=t+1
75 if g>r then 90
80 print "Too low. Try again"
85 goto 40
90 print "Too high.  Try again."
95 goto 40
100 r=rnd(0)
105 r=r%100+1
110 return
```

Enter "run" and play the game.

Immediately the slow speed of execution becomes apparent. Going from assembly to Tiny BASIC we have sacrificed ease of programming for speed. In the next chapter, we look at some extensions of Tiny BASIC that improve both speed and capability.

Chapter 14
Tiny BASIC Extended (TBX)

Back in the 1970's, when I first published a version of Tiny BASIC, I included several enhancements and called the version "Tiny BASIC Extended" or TBX for short. In this chapter, we add some of these enhancements to Tiny BASIC.

Preprocessing Program Lines

BASIC is classified as an "interpretive" language because it executes directly from program text without first compiling it into machine language. As a matter of fact, most BASIC interpreters do some preprocessing of program lines, so they are not strictly working from ASCII text. Tiny BASIC is no exception. We saw early on that we could improve GOTO and GOSUB search speed by converting the ASCII line number to a 2-byte binary value and adding it along with the line length to the beginning of each program line.

Another speed limiting factor in Tiny BASIC is the time it takes to search the keyword table before a command or statement can be processed. To increase execution speed in TBX, we move the lookup to when the program line is first entered and replace the keyword with a single byte *keyword code*.

The keyword code is equal to the numeric position of the keyword in the Keyword Table (starting at 0) with the MS bit set. Setting the MS bit uniquely identifies the byte as a keyword code, since no other bytes in the ASCII text area have the MS bit set.

Here is an example line of code from Tiny BASIC and TBX showing the additional keyword preprocessing.

10 LET A=I+1:PRINT A

Tiny BASIC (in hex): 00 0A 12 20 4c 45 54 20 41 3d 49 2b 31 3a 50 52 49 4e 54 20 41 0d

TBX (in hex): 00 0a 0e 20 <u>81</u> 20 41 3d 49 2b 31 3a <u>87</u> 20 41 0d

"LET" and "PRINT" have been replaced by "0x81" and "0x87", respectively. In TBX, "LET" is the second item in the Keyword Table, so its keyword code is "0x81". "PRINT" is number 8, so its keyword code is "0x87". At execution time, TBX uses the keyword code to do a simple lookup in the Keyword Link Table to get the execution address for the LET and PRINT statements. Thus, the time-consuming table look-up during execution is eliminated!

Note: In Tiny BASIC, we put LET near the start of the keyword table so it would be found quickly. Then, when omitting LET, we cancelled this advantage by having to search the entire keyword table before determining an optional LET! In TBX, if the MS bit is not set at the beginning of a statement, we immediately assume optional LET, eliminating the execution speed penalty.

In the warm start code below, we place the "trns" subroutine immediately after the "getline" subroutine so that keywords in the inputted line are translated to keyword codes before any line editing or processing occurs.

```
wstart: call    winit          ;Initialize for warm start
        mvi     a,0b00000011   ;Reset push/pop & call/return sta
        out     0xff,a
        call    newline        ;New line
        call    getline        ;Get command or statement
  ➤     call    trns           ;Translate keywords
        call    newline        ;New line
        call    tstl           ;Command or statement (to insert
        jnc     cmdpr          ;If a command, go execute it
        call    insrt          ;If a statement, insert it (or delete
        jmp     wstart         ;Repeat
```

Here is Part 1 the "trns" code.

(Next page please)

```
;
; Translate Input Line
;
1   trns:       lxi     iram,bufstrt        ;Point IRAM to input buffer start
            mvi     h,hi(bufstrt)       ;Point HL to input buffer start
            mvi     l,lo(bufstrt)
2   trnsl0:     ldx     a,(iram)            ;Get byte
            cpi     a,cr                ;Reached end of line?
            jz      trnse               ;If so, done
3           cpi     a,'"'               ;A literal?
            jz      trnsc1              ;If so, copy it ignoring text
4           push    a                   ;Check for keyword
            push    h
            push    l
            call    getkey              ;Is it a keyword?
            pop     l
            pop     h
            pop     a
            jnc     trnsc0              ;If not, copy byte as is
            adi     c,0b10000000        ;If a keyword, set MS bit
            mov     m,c                 ;Store it back in input buffer
            adi     l,1                 ;Increment HL
            aci     h,0
            jmp     trnsl0              ;Process next byte
```

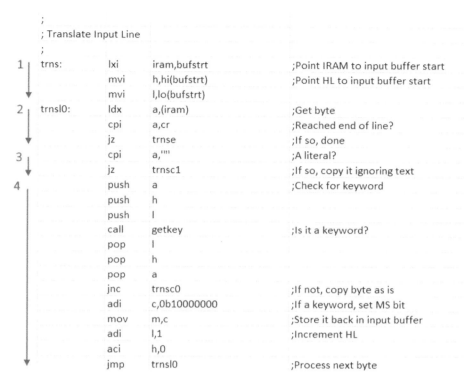

1. We load both HL and IRAM with the address of the input buffer.

2. We check if the end-of-line CR has been reached and if so, store the CR and return.

3. Within literals, we ignore keywords. This code segment checks for a quotation mark and, if found, branches to code that ignores the literal.

4. We call "getkey" subroutine to check for a valid keyword. If found, "geykey" returns with carry set and the keyword code in the C register. We store the keyword code with MS bit set in the input buffer replacing the original keyword.

Note: Since registers A, H, and L are in use before calling "getkey", they must be preserved using PUSHs and POPs.

Now for Part 2.

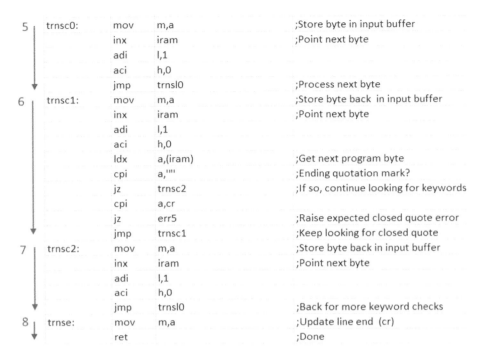

```
5   trnsc0:    mov    m,a            ;Store byte in input buffer
                inx    iram           ;Point next byte
                adi    l,1
                aci    h,0
                jmp    trnsl0         ;Process next byte
6   trnsc1:     mov    m,a            ;Store byte back in input buffer
                inx    iram           ;Point next byte
                adi    l,1
                aci    h,0
                ldx    a,(iram)       ;Get next program byte
                cpi    a,'"'          ;Ending quotation mark?
                jz     trnsc2         ;If so, continue looking for keywords
                cpi    a,cr
                jz     err5           ;Raise expected closed quote error
                jmp    trnsc1         ;Keep looking for closed quote
7   trnsc2:     mov    m,a            ;Store byte back in input buffer
                inx    iram           ;Point next byte
                adi    l,1
                aci    h,0
                jmp    trnsl0         ;Back for more keyword checks
8   trnse:      mov    m,a            ;Update line end (cr)
                ret                   ;Done
```

5. If no keyword is found, the character is stored, and we jump back for another character.

6 & 7. This code reads and stores literal text including the closing quotation mark.

8. This is the exit point of the subroutine. The CR character is added to the end of the TBX line before returning to the calling routine.

Note: We can modify the inputted line <u>in place</u> because the keyword code is always shorter than the keyword it replaces.

Multi-Statement Lines

Including more than one statement on a line not only saves space, it executes faster since the processing overhead in the "done" routine is avoided. We use a colon ":" as the multiple statements separator. Consider this snippet from the High/Low Guessing Game program.

102

```
10 PRINT
20 PRINT "High/Low Guessing Game"
30 PRINT
40 . . .
```

Changing to a multi-statement line we have:

```
10 PRINT: PRINT "High/Low Guessing Game":PRINT
```

Besides increased execution speed, combining related statements on a multi-statement line can improve readability; i.e., the ease with which a human reader can comprehend the purpose, flow, and function of the code.

These code changes to Tiny BASIC were made.

(Next page please)

```
1   done:      inp    a,cntr_port        ;Get keyboard character into A
               ani    a,kby_mask         ;Character available?
               jz     donec0             ;If not, continue
               inp    a,data_port        ;Get the ASCII character
               cpi    a,escape           ;Escape code?
               jz     wstart             ;If so, do a warm boot
    donec0:    call   skipspace          ;Skip any spaces
               cpi    a,':'              ;End of multi-statement (:)?
               jz     stmprns            ;If so, go on to next statement
               cpi    a,cr               ;End of line (CR)?
               jnz    err4               ;If not, raise expected end of line error
               cpi    a,cr               ;End of line (CR)?
               jnz    err4               ;If not, raise expected end of line error
    donec0a:   inx    iram

2   printe:    call   skipspace          ;Get first non-space character
               cpi    a,cr               ;End of line?
               jz     done               ;If so, done w/o new line
               cpi    a,':'              ;Multistatement line? (TBX Mod)
               jz     done               ;If so, done w/o new line (TBX Mod)

3   printc2:   cpi    a,cr               ;End of line?
               jz     printc3            ;If so, continue  TBX Start
               cpi    a,':'              ;Multistatement line?
               jz     printc3            ;If so, continue

4   returnl:   ldx    a,(iram)           ;Find CR
               cpi    a,cr
               jz     done               ;If found, then done
               cpi    a,':'              ;TBX
               jz     done
```

1. Except in the "done" routine, we simply check for a colon as we did for the CR and handle it the same way. In the "done" routine, a colon is treated differently. For the colon, we jump directly into the statement processing routine avoiding the line number update and end of memory check that occurs with a CR.

2, 3, and 4. For the PRINT and return statements, the colon is treated the same as a carriage return.

Note: The "ifdone" code was not changed, so it searches only for a CR. Thus, when an "IF…THEN" statement encounters a false result, multi-statements beyond THEN are ignored.

Data Arrays

Computer arrays in general are multidimensional. To keep things simple, we implement only single dimensional arrays. The "DIM var(n)" statement reconfigures A to Z variable "var" as an array. The array index "n" ranges from 0 to n making a total of n+1 array values or *elements*. For example, "DIM V(512)" creates array "V" consisting of 513 array elements each of which can store a 16-bit value.

When dimensioned as an array variable, the original variable location in Data RAM is used to store an address pointer to the reserved area in Data RAM where the array values are stored.

Note: To keep things simple, we do not store the dimension size "n", so the programmer must assume responsibility for not exceeding array bounds.

Array memory is located above "prgend" in Data RAM. When the DIM statement is executed, we zero all array elements. To dimension more than one array at a time, we separate array variables by commas as "DIM (10), B(100)".

Part 1 of the "DIM" statement code is shown below.

(Next page please)

```
;
; DIM Processor TBX
;
dim:        call    skipspace            ;Point to variable
            adi     a,0xc0               ;A-Z or a-z?
            jnc     err7                 ;If not, raise expected variable error
            inx     iram                 ;Point next program byte
            ani     a,0b00011111         ;Mask lower bits
            dcr     a                    ;Adjust to zero base
            rlc     a                    ;Multiply by 2
            mvi     l,lo(varstrt)        ;Calculate variable's address
            mvi     h,hi(varstrt)
            add     l,a
            aci     h,0
            push    h                    ;Put variable's address on stack
            push    l
            ldr     l,arrystrt           ;Get array start in HL
            ldr     h,arrystrt+1
            push    h                    ;Put on PP stack
            push    l
            call    store                ;Store array start at variable's address
            ldx     a,(iram)             ;Open prenthesis?
            cpi     a,'('
            jnz     err0                 ;If not, raise syntax error
            inx     iram                 ;Point next byte
            call    expr                 ;Get array's dimension
            ldr     l,arrystrt           ;Get array start address in HL
            ldr     h,arrystrt+1
            pop     e                    ;Pop array's dimension in DE
            pop     d
            call    skipspace            ;Get program byte
            cpi     a,')'                ;Should be closed parenthesis?
            jnz     err0                 ;If not, raise a syntax error
```

1. With the variable name (A to Z) loaded in the A register, we calculate its address and push the address onto the PP Stack.

2. Next we get the current array start address and push it onto the PP Stack. We call "store" that stores the array start address in the variable.

Note: There is nothing to indicate that the variable is an array. It's simply a 16-bit value that happens to be the array start address. Later, we use an open parenthesis following the variable name to indicate that this value is an address link into a data array.

3. In this code segment, we calculate the dimension or size of the array. The code includes checks for open and close parentheses and uses the 'expr' subroutine to get the dimension. At exit, the dimension is on the PP Stack.

Note: While the dimension is usually a constant, "expr" allows it to be a calculated value including variables.

Now for part 2 of the DIM code.

```
4          inx    iram              ;Point next program byte
           rlc    e                 ;Double array's dimenion
           ral    d
           jc     err15             ;Raise out of memory error
           add    e,l               ;Calculate new array start address
           adc    d,h
           jc     err15             ;If carry, raise out of memory error.
           cpi    d,hi(memend)      ;Check out of memory?
           jnc    err15             ;If so, raise out of memory error
           str    arrystrt,e        ;Store new array start address
           str    arrystrt+1,d
5  diml:   mvi    m,0               ;Zero array memory
           adi    l,1               ;Point next array byte
           aci    h,0
           cmp    l,e               ;Done?
           jnz    diml              ;If not, back for another
           cmp    h,d
           jnz    diml              ;If not, back for another
6          call   skipspace         ;Get next program byte
           cpi    a,','             ;More variables to dimension?
           jnz    done              ;If not, then done
           inx    iram              ;Point next program byte
           jmp    dim               ;Process another variable
```

4. Since the memory required for an array is double the dimension, we multiply the dimension by 2 and add the result to the original array starting address. We also check to be sure that the size of the array does not exceed Data RAM's capacity.

5. We zero all array elements.

6. In the final code segment, we check for a comma indicating that another array is to be dimensioned. If so, we jump back to the beginning of DIM code. Otherwise, we are done.

Logical Expression Evaluation

In Tiny BASIC's IF statement, we evaluated a simple relational expression by comparing two expressions using relational operators "<", ">", and "=". For TBX, we expand this evaluation to a logical expression by adding the AND operator "&", the OR operator "|", and the NOT operator "!". The order of operation is NOT, AND, then OR. As with Tiny BASIC expressions, parentheses can be added to change the order of operations. Logical expression code below parallels closely the design of the Tiny BASIC expression routine "expr".

Here is part 1.

(Next page please)

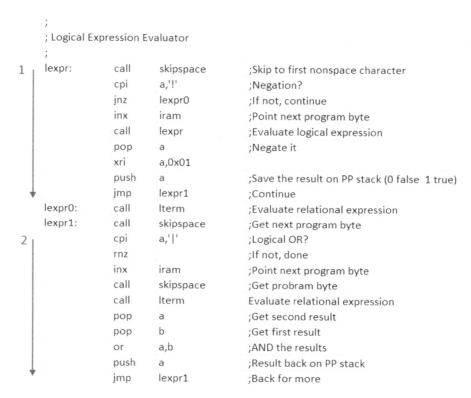

```
;
; Logical Expression Evaluator
;
lexpr:      call    skipspace       ;Skip to first nonspace character
            cpi     a,'!'           ;Negation?
            jnz     lexpr0          ;If not, continue
            inx     iram            ;Point next program byte
            call    lexpr           ;Evaluate logical expression
            pop     a               ;Negate it
            xri     a,0x01
            push    a               ;Save the result on PP stack (0 false  1 true)
            jmp     lexpr1          ;Continue
lexpr0:     call    lterm           ;Evaluate relational expression
lexpr1:     call    skipspace       ;Get next program byte
            cpi     a,'|'           ;Logical OR?
            rnz                     ;If not, done
            inx     iram            ;Point next program byte
            call    skipspace       ;Get probram byte
            call    lterm           Evaluate relational expression
            pop     a               ;Get second result
            pop     b               ;Get first result
            or      a,b             ;AND the results
            push    a               ;Result back on PP stack
            jmp     lexpr1          ;Back for more
```

1. As already noted, we follow the expression code with logical operators replacing the arithmetic operators. Notice that we use the PP Stack to temporarily store the logical result with a numeric "1" representing "True" and "0" false. We also modified the relational expression code to leave a "1" or "0" on the PP Stack instead of returning with carry status set or reset. For the NOT operation, the evaluated logical expression leaves a "1" or "0" on the PP Stack and the XRI instruction inverts it to carry out the negate operation.

2. Logical operator precedence follows the arithmetic equivalent with AND first and OR next then left to right unless modified by parentheses. Logical terms are separated by ORs and factors by ANDs. In this code, we handle OR operations using the CPU's OR instruction.

And now part 2.

```
;
lterm:      call    lfactor
lterm0:     call    skipspace       ;Get next program byte
            cpi     a,'&'           ;Logical AND?
            rnz                     ;If not, done
            inx     iram            ;Point next program byte
            call    skipspace       ;Get program byte
            call    lfactor         ;Evaluate relational expression
            pop     a               ;Get second result
            pop     b               ;Get first result
            and     a,b             ;OR the results
            push    a               ;Result back on PP stack
            jmp     lterm0          ;Back for more
;
lfactor:    call    skipspace       ;Get next program byte
            cpi     a,'('           ;Is it an open parenthsis
            jnz     rexpr           ;If not, continue
            inx     iram            ;If so, evaluate the logical expression
            call    lexpr
            call    skipspace       ;Should be a closed parenthesis?
            cpi     a,')'
            jnz     err14           ;If not, raise a missing parenthesis error
            inx     iram            If so, point the next byte and done
            ret
```

3. We evaluate logical factors separated by ANDs using the CPU's AND instruction.

4. In "lfactor" code, we first check for parentheses and if found, recursively calls "lexpr". Otherwise, we call the relational expression subroutine and its result is pushed onto the PP Stack.

IF...THEN Extension

Tiny BASIC's "IF...THEN" accepted at line number after "THEN" as the True option target. This was done by making THEN's processing routine the same as GOTO's. In TBX, we introduce a separate routine for "THEN".

```
;
; IF Processor
;
if:         call    lexpr           ;Evaluate logical expression
            pop     a               ;Get logical result
            rrc     a               ;Rotate into carry
            jc      stmprc          ;If TRUE, process THEN
ifdone:     ldx     a,(iram)        ;Find CR
            cpi     a,cr
            jz      done            ;If found, then done
            inx     iram
            jmp     ifdone
```

1. We replace the relational evaluation code a call to "lexpr". The true or false result is determined by a "1" or "0" respectively on the PP Stack. We pop the result into register A and rotate it into carry. Carry equal to "1" indicates a true result and we process the "THEN" statement.

2. This code is unchanged; it skips to the end of the line as before.

In the Tiny BASIC, THEN was process exactly as a GOTO. In TBX, we go a step farther; a statement can also follow THEN. Here is the modified THEN code.

```
;
; THEN Processor TBX
;
then:       call    skipspace       ;Get next program byte
            call    chknum          ;Is numeric?
            jc      goto            ;If so, then process GOTO
            jmp     stmprc          ;Otherwise, process statement
```

1. We skip any spaces then check if a line number is present. If so, we process it just as with a GOTO. This maintains backward compatibility to the original Tiny BASIC.

2. If not a line number, we assume it's a statement (any statement!) and process it.

Below is an example program that demonstrates logical expression evaluation.

```
10 INPUT a:INPUT b:INPUT c
20 IF c=2 | a=1 & b=1 THEN PRINT "yes":GOTO 10
30 PRINT "no":GOTO 10

>run

?2
?3
?2
yes
?1
?1
?3
yes
?2
?2
?3
no
?
```

Tiny BASIC would have ignored the order of operations and performed the OR "|" operation first. With our new code the AND "&" gets precedence.

RPT – Repeat Statement

One of the advantages of creating your custom version of a language is the ability to devise custom commands and statements. The RPT (Repeat) statement is an example. To create loops with Tiny BASIC, we would ordinarily use IF..THEN and GOTO statements. The RPT statement accomplishes the same thing taking advantage of multi-statement lines. Consider this example that prints numbers from 1 to 10.

In Tiny BASIC,

10 i=0
20 PRINT I
30 I=I+1
40 if I<=10 THEN 20
50 STOP

In TBX,

```
10 I=0
20 I=I+1:PRINT I:RPT I<=10
30 STOP
```

"RPT lexpr" repeats statements on a line as long as the logical expression "lexpr" is true. The TBX example produces the same result as Tiny BASIC but with one distinct advantage. The RPT statement loop does not have to search for a line number as in Tiny BASIC's "IF..THEN" statement. The result is faster execution with the RPT loop!

Multilevel loops are also possible. See the example below.

In Tiny BASIC,

```
5 DIM D100)
10 J=0
20 I=0
30 D(I+50*J)=1
40 J=J+1:IF J<50 THEN 30
50 I=I+1:IFJj<50 THEN 20
60 STOP
```

In TBX,

```
5 DIM D(100)
10 J=0
20 i=0
30 D(J+50*J)=1:J=J+1:RTP J<50:J=0:I=I+1:RPT I<50
40 STOP
```

In the Tiny BASIC example, array variable D is initialized to 1 using conventional Tiny BASIC coding. By using two index variables, we treat the array as two dimensional of size 50 by 50 with "I" the row and "J" is column. The TBX example accomplishes the same task without searching for a line number during each iteration.

If no logical expression appears after RPT, the looping continues indefinitely. In such a case, an IF statement within the repeated code could provide an exit.

Here is the RPT code.

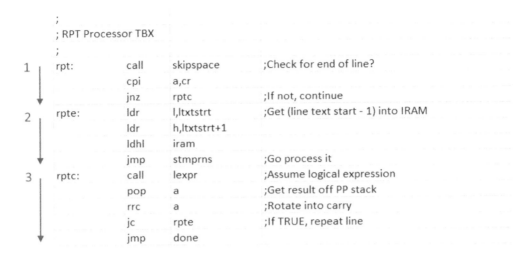

```
;
; RPT Processor TBX
;
1   rpt:      call    skipspace       ;Check for end of line?
              cpi     a,cr
              jnz     rptc            ;If not, continue
2   rpte:     ldr     l,ltxtstrt      ;Get (line text start - 1) into IRAM
              ldr     h,ltxtstrt+1
              ldhl    iram
              jmp     stmprns         ;Go process it
3   rptc:     call    lexpr           ;Assume logical expression
              pop     a               ;Get result off PP stack
              rrc     a               ;Rotate into carry
              jc      rpte            ;If TRUE, repeat line
              jmp     done
```

1 & 2. In "stmpr", we store the address of the text immediately following the line number in "ltxtstrt" and "ltxtstrt+1". This makes it possible to transfer execution back to the start of the keyword when the "RPT" statement is found. In this code segment, we load the "itxtstrt" address into IRAM, bypass DONE and transfer execution back to the beginning of the line.

3. We execute this code when a logical expression is found. On a true result (a "1" on the PP Stack), we transfer execution to the beginning of the line. For a false (a "0" on the PP Stack), we send the code to "done" and execute the next statement following a ":" or CR.

Data Statement

In traditional BASIC, we use a combination of READ and DATA statements to import numerical data into variables. I have always disliked this approach because the READ and DATA statements are generally in different parts of the BASIC program leading to confusion as to what DATA is matched with what READ. With the ability to customize TBX, I experimented with a different approach. The TBX READ statement looks like this:

Lne_num READ var=data0,data1,...

For simple variables, it is no different from a LET. The real difference shows up with arrays. Consider the code below that loads data into a 10 element array A.

114

10 READ A(0)= 1,2,3,4,5,6,7,8,9,10

After execution, A(0) = 1, A(1) = 2, . . . , A(9) =10. The variable specifies the starting element for the data array read with subsequent values stored in consecutive array elements. This approach keeps the variables adjacent to their data, producing self-documenting code.

We can use READ/DATA statements to process multiple sets of data. In this case, the program reads one set of data, processes it, then read another set until an end-of-data marker is reached. The TBX READ statement can accomplish the same task using the calculated GOSUB feature. Consider the program below.

```
10 DIM A(3)
20 I=100
30 GOSUB(I)
40 IF A(0)=0 THEN GOTO 99
50 PRINT A(0),A(1),A(2)
60 I=I+5:GOTO 30
99 STOP
100 READ A(0)= 1,2,3:RETURN
105 READ A(0)=4,5,6:RETURN
110 READ A(0)=7,8,9:RETURN
115 READ A(0)=0:RETURN
```

In Line 30, the GOSUB line number is the value of variable "I", which is 100, 105, etc. The subroutine in each case is a READ statement that populates array variable "A" with a unique set of values. Each data set is printed then the next value is read. When line 115 is read, the "0" value returned in A(0) results in a transfer to the STOP statement. The programs output looks like this:

```
>run

1          2          3
4          5          6
7          8          9

STOP at line 99
>|
```

The READ code is shown below.

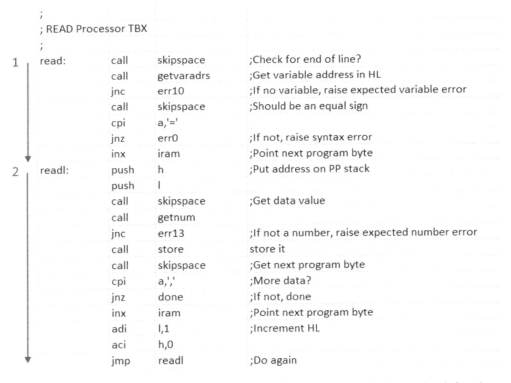

```
        ;
        ; READ Processor TBX
        ;
1   read:      call    skipspace    ;Check for end of line?
               call    getvaradrs   ;Get variable address in HL
               jnc     err10        ;If no variable, raise expected variable error
               call    skipspace    ;Should be an equal sign
               cpi     a,'='
               jnz     err0         ;If not, raise syntax error
               inx     iram         ;Point next program byte
2   readl:     push    h            ;Put address on PP stack
               push    l
               call    skipspace    ;Get data value
               call    getnum
               jnc     err13        ;If not a number, raise expected number error
               call    store        store it
               call    skipspace    ;Get next program byte
               cpi     a,','        ;More data?
               jnz     done         ;If not, done
               inx     iram         ;Point next program byte
               adi     l,1          ;Increment HL
               aci     h,0
               jmp     readl        ;Do again
```

1. We call "getvaradrs" to load the address of the variable in HL then check for the "=" sign.

2. We push the current variable address in HL onto the PP Stack. Using the "getnum" subroutine, we put the first value onto the PP Stack, then store it at the variable address. If no comma is found, the routine ends. Finding a comma indicates more data and we pass back the next variable address now in HL to the start of this segment.

Note: This code assumes that when HL is incremented twice, it points to the next variable address. This obviously works fine with arrays. For simple variables, the "next variable address" is that of the next alphabetic variable. Thus, "READ A= 1,2,3" would result in "1" stored in A, "2" in B, and "3" in C. This is not something we would likely use; it's just an extra "feature" of the code design.

In the next chapter, we see how to customize TBX further by adding a new statement and function.

Chapter 15
Adding TBX Keywords

In this chapter, we show how to add keywords that represent new statements and functions. In this case, we add a new statement "POKE" and a new function "PEEK" to TBX. "POKE adrs,byte" stores the "byte" value at address "adrs" in Data RAM. When it appears as a function in an expression, "PEEK(adrs)" returns the value of the byte at address "adrs" in Data RAM.

Note: POKE may raise an eyebrow for some readers because it allows the user to change Data RAM from within a TBX program. Doing so, could prove disastrous if TBX itself is poked!

Modifying Keyword Tables

Anytime a new keyword is added, the keyword tables must be changed. The first table contains the ASCII text of each keyword.

(Next page please)

```
;
; Keyword Table
;
keytbl:    db        'R','P','T'+128
           db        'L','E','T'+128
           db        'I','F'+128
           db        'T','H','E','N'+128
           db        'G','O','T','O'+128
           db        'G','O','S','U','B'+128
           db        'R','E','T','U','R','N'+128
           db        'P','R','I','N','T'+128
           db        'I','N','P','U','T'+128
           db        'R','U','N'+128
           db        'R','E','M'+128
           db        'D','I','M'+128
           db        'R','E','A','D'+128
           db        'C','L','R'+128
           db        'L','I','S','T'+128
           db        'S','T','O','P'+128
           db        'N','E','W'+128
           db        'L','O','A','D'+128
           db        'R','N','D'+128
   ───────▶ db        'P','O','K','E'+128
   ───────▶ db        'P','E','E','K'+128
           db        0
```

We added the two new keywords as shown. Adding 128 (0b10000000) to the last letter sets the MS bit.

The second table has the same order with a 2-byte address for each entry. For statements and commands, we use the label address of the processing routine. For functions, we raise a syntax error because they are not executable, only appearing in TBX expressions.

```
;
; Keyword Link Table
;
linktbl:    db      lo(rpt),hi(rpt)         ;RPT-REPEAT
            db      lo(let),hi(let)         ;LET
            db      lo(if),hi(if)           ;IF
            db      lo(then),hi(then)       ;THEN
            db      lo(goto),hi(goto)       ;GOTO
            db      lo(gosub),hi(gosub)     ;GOSUB
            db      lo(return),hi(return)   ;RETURN
            db      lo(print),hi(print)     ;PRINT
            db      lo(input),hi(input)     ;INPUT
            db      lo(run),hi(run)         ;RUN
            db      lo(rem),hi(rem)         ;REM
            db      lo(dim),hi(dim)         ;DIM
            db      lo(read),hi(read)       ;DIM
            db      lo(clr),hi(clr)         ;DIM
            db      lo(list),hi(list)       ;LIST
            db      lo(stop),hi(stop)       ;STOP
            db      lo(new),hi(new)         ;NEW
            db      lo(load),hi(load)       ;LOAD
rndlink:    db      lo(err0),hi(err0)       ;RND Function
            db      lo(poke),hi(poke)       ;POKE         <--
peeklink:   db      lo(err0),hi(err0)       ;PEEK Function<--
;
random      equ     (rndlink-linktbl)/2
peekid      equ     (peeklink-linktbl)/2                 <--
;
```

The arrows show the newly inserted lines. The first two arrows are address pointers. "POKE" is a statement, so we use its processing address label. For "PEEK" a function, we use "err0" to raise a syntax error. At the third arrow, we calculate the keyword codes "random" and "peekid" for RND and PEEK, respectively. We use these below to identify the function in the "expr" subroutine.

Adding New Statement POKE

For routines like POKE, we add the processing code in line with other routines. Here is the "poke" routine.

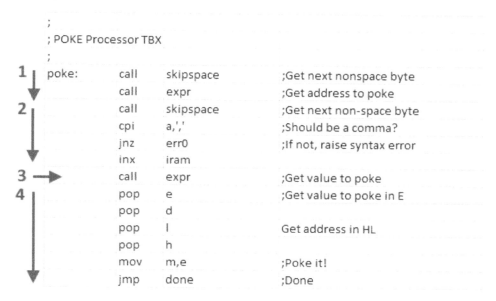

```
;
; POKE Processor TBX
;
poke:      call     skipspace          ;Get next nonspace byte
           call     expr               ;Get address to poke
           call     skipspace          ;Get next non-space byte
           cpi      a,','              ;Should be a comma?
           jnz      err0               ;If not, raise syntax error
           inx      iram
           call     expr               ;Get value to poke
           pop      e                  ;Get value to poke in E
           pop      d
           pop      l                  Get address in HL
           pop      h
           mov      m,e                ;Poke it!
           jmp      done               ;Done
```

1. After skipping to the first non-space, we call "expr" to get the address to poke.

2. We skip spaces and check for the required comma and raise a syntax error if its isn't found.

3. We call "expr" again to get the byte value to be stored in the poke address.

4. After retrieving the byte value in DE and the address in HL, we store E to Data RAM at HL. (The Data RAM is 8-bits wide, so we ignore the D value.)

Adding New Function PEEK

Functions are processed within Tiny BASIC's "expr" subroutine. See the code segment below.

```
factor:      call    getfnct  ◄——        ;Is it a function?
             rc                           If so, put on PP stack and return
             call    getvar               ;Is it a number?
             rc                           ;If so, put on PP stack and return
             call    getnum               ;Is it a variable?
             rc                           ;If so, put on PP stack and return

      • • •

;
; Get Function Value on PP Stack
;
1 getfnct:    ldx    a,(iram)             ;Get key number in A
             ani     a,0b01111111         ;Mask off MS bit
2            cpi     a,random             ;Is it RND?
             jz      rndm                 ;If so, process it
             cpi     a,peekid             ;Is it PEEK?
             jz      peek                 ;If so, process it
3            sub     a,a                  ;Reset carry and return
             ret
```

In the "factor" segment of "expr", we call "getfnct" to check if IRAM points to a function. If so, we push the function value the PP Stack and return with carry set.

1. We mask off the MS bit of the keyword code.

2. We check for the functions and branch accordingly.

3. If no function is identified, we reset the carry and return.

The "peek" code is given below.

```
;
; PEEK Function
;
```

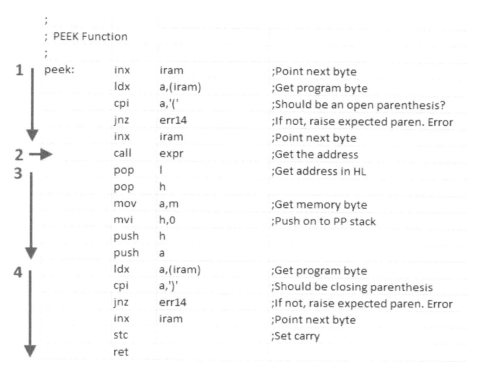

```
1   peek:      inx    iram            ;Point next byte
               ldx    a,(iram)        ;Get program byte
               cpi    a,'('           ;Should be an open parenthesis?
               jnz    err14           ;If not, raise expected paren. Error
               inx    iram            ;Point next byte
2 →            call   expr            ;Get the address
3              pop    l               ;Get address in HL
               pop    h
               mov    a,m             ;Get memory byte
               mvi    h,0             ;Push on to PP stack
               push   h
               push   a
4              ldx    a,(iram)        ;Get program byte
               cpi    a,')'           ;Should be closing parenthesis
               jnz    err14           ;If not, raise expected paren. Error
               inx    iram            ;Point next byte
               stc                    ;Set carry
               ret
```

1. We check for the required open parenthesis.

2. We call "expr" to get the address to inspect and push it onto the PP Stack.

3. We pop the address into HL then load the "peek" memory byte into register A. We push a 0x00 (in H) then A onto the PP Stack.

4. We check for a closing parenthesis, set carry to indicate function was found, and return.

In the next chapter, we exercise these changes by programming Conway's Game of Life.

Chapter 16
Testing TBX

In chapter 3, we tested Tiny BASIC using the High/Low Guessing Game. On the left below is the Tiny BASIC listing with some minor changes. On the right, is the revised Tiny BASIC Extended version that takes advantage of multi-statement lines.

Tiny BASIC

```
5 e=rnd(1)
10 print
15 print "High/Low Guessing Game"
20 print
25 e=rnd(0)%100+1
30 t=0
35 print "I am thinking of a number between 1 and 100."
40 t=t+1
45 print "Your guess";
50 input g
55 if g>e then 75
60 if g<e then 85
65 print "You got it in ";t;"tries"
70 goto 10
75 print "Too high. Try again."
80 goto 40
85 print "Too low. Try again"
90 goto 40
```

Tiny BASIC Extended

```
5 e=rnd(1)
10 print:print "High/Low Guessing Game":print
15 e=rnd(0)%100+1
20 t=0
25 print "I am thinking of a number between 1 and 100."
30 t=t+1:print "Your guess";:input g
35 if g=e then print "You got it in ";t;"tries":goto 10
40 if g>e then print "Too high.  Try again.":goto 30
45 print "Too low. Try again":goto 30
```

Improved Readability

To begin, let's consider TBX's improved readability; i.e., the ease with which a human reader can comprehend the purpose, logic, and flow of the code.

1. Lines 10 to 20 in the original print the title. We combine them by purpose in line 10 of the revised version.

2. Counting guesses as a guess is input makes logical sense, so we combine lines 40 and 45 into line 30.

3. Lines 65 to 90 are compressed into lines 35 to 45 by taking advantage of the "THEN" statement processing option. Each new line is logically complete improving readability.

Improved Speed

Let's look at speed improvement. Below is a short test program that counts from 0 to 100. Shown are Logisim timings for TB and TBX. (Tick Frequency is 4.1 kHz.)

1 TB	2 TB	3 TBX	4 TBX
10 x=0	10 x=0	10 x=0	10 x=0
20 x=x+1	20 let x=x+1	20 x=x+1	20 x=x+1:rpt x<100
30 if x<100 then 20	30 if x<100 then 20	30 if x<100 goto 20	
10m 0 s	8m 50s	2m 20s	1m 38s

1. This is the worst case when TB must look through the entire Keyword Table before recognizing the omitted LET statement.

2. A slightly better TB speed results when LET is not omitted. With LET keyword close to the front of the Keyword Table, it is found quickly.

3. TBX's prepossessing shines here. Using Keyword Codes, we do away with Keyword Table lookup during execution. We see a factor of four improvement!

4. Finally, the RPT statement almost halves the time again by eliminating the search for line 20.

Conway's Game of Life

The improvement of TBX over TB is impressive but Logisim is still painfully slow. Whenever I am experimenting with CPU design or language development, I use John Conway's Game of Life as a benchmark for execution speed. My version of the Life is based on a 16 by 16 matrix of cells where living cells are indicted by an asterisk. Initially, a pattern of live cells is placed in the matrix. For each generation of life, the following rules are applied:

1. Any live cell with fewer than two live neighbors dies, as if by underpopulation.

2. Any live cell with two or three live neighbors lives on to the next generation.

3. Any live cell with more than three live neighbors dies, as if by overpopulation.

4. Any dead cell with exactly three live neighbors becomes a live cell, as if by reproduction.

The thousands of steps in processing a single generation of cells takes considerable CPU time. In fact, Logisim is not practical test bed, as each generation takes tens of minutes.

Testing on the Cyclone V FPGA makes more sense. In fact, TBX Life speed tests done on the Cyclone V FPGA implementation of the BYOC-24 exceed 100 generation per minute!

Let's look at the TBX version of the game and consider how we can use TBX's extensions to advantage.

Here is Part 1 of the original TBX version of Game of Life with a brief description of its components.

```
 1    5 DIM V(512)
     10 B=0:GOSUB 900:CLR
 2   15 B=B+1:GOSUB 800
     20 GOSUB 700
     70 M=0
     80 N=0
     90 A=0
    100 I=M-1
    110 J=N-1
    120 GOSUB 200:J=J+1:IF J<=N+1 THEN GOTO 120
    130 I=I+1: IF I<=M+1 THEN GOTO 110
    140 GOSUB 300
    150 N=N+1:IF N<=15 THEN GOTO 90
    160 M=M+1:IF M<=15 THEN GOTO 80
    170 GOTO 15
 3  200 IF I=M THEN IF J=N THEN RETURN
    205 K=I+16:L=J
    210 IF K<16 THEN K=31
    215 IF K>31 THEN K=16
    220 IF J<0 THEN L=15
    225 IF J>15 THEN L=0
    230 A=A+V(16*K+L)
    240 RETURN
```

1. This is the "Setup" code. In line 5, the DIM(512) reserves space for two 16 by 16 arrays. Call them Array 0 and Array 1. In line 10 we zero the generations variable B, load Array 0 with the initial pattern (see item 7 below) and clear the display.

126

2. This is the "Main Routine". We start in line 15 by incrementing the generation and printing Array 0 (see item 6 below). In line 20, we copy Array 0 to Array 1. We use Array 1 when applying the Game of Life rules and make changes to Array 0. Lines 70 to 170 perform the scan of Array 0 counting live cells around each cell. (See item 3.) Line 140 applies the Game of Life rules and updates the cell in Array 1. (See item 4.)

3. Subroutine 200 counts the live cells surrounding the target cell (row I and column k of Array 0). Notice that we have assumed the left and right edges of the array are stitched together as are the top and bottom edges. This is called a *toroidal array*. The result is that live cell areas move across a field edge and reappear at the opposite edge.

Here is Part 2 of the Game of Life.

```
4  300 IF V(16*M+N)=0 THEN IF A=3 THEN V(16*M+N)=1
   305 IF V(16*M+N)=1 THEN IF A<2 THEN V(16*M+N)=0
   310 IF V(16*M+N)=1 THEN IF A>3 THEN V(16*M+N)=0
   315 RETURN
5  700 I=16:J=0
   705 C=0
   710 V(16*I+C)=V(16*J+C):C=C+1:IF C<15 THEN GOTO 710
   715 I=I+1:J=J+1:IF J<15 THEN GOTO 705
   720 RETURN
6  800 PRINT
   810 M=0
   815 N=0
   820 IF V(16*M+N)=0 THEN PRINT " ";:GOTO 830
   825 PRINT "*";
   830 N=N+1:IF N<15 THEN GOTO 820
   835 PRINT
   840 M=M+1: IF M<15 THEN GOTO 815
   845 PRINT "GEN ";B
   850 RETURN
7  900 I=5:J=7:V(16*I+J)=1
   910 I=6:J=6:V(16*I+J)=1:J=7:V(16*I+J)=1:J=8:V(16*I+J)=1
   920 I=7:J=6:V(16*I+J)=1:J=8:V(16*I+J)=1
   930 I=8:J=6:V(16*I+J)=1:J=7:V(16*I+J)=1:J=8:V(16*I+J)=1
   940 I=9:J=7:V(16*I+J)=1
   950 RETURN
```

4. Subroutine 300 applies the Game of Life rules using a series of IF statements: Line 300 - Rule 4; line 305 – Rule 1; line 310 – Rule 3. Rule 2 is a consequence of Rules 1 and 3 and needs no check.

5. Subroutine 700 copies Array 0 to Array 1.

6. Subroutine 800 prints Array 0. A dead cell is printed as space and a live cell, an asterisk.

7. Subroutine 900 initials Array 0 with the starting pattern. When an array is dimensioned, all elements are zero. To create the pattern, we store 1s in the array. Recall that TBX array elements are numbered beginning with 0.

Our purpose here is not to describe the program in detail but show improvements that can be made using TBX's extensions. To begin, let's look at data arrays.

1. Data Arrays – We could not program Life in Tiny BASIC because it doesn't support arrays. In the TBX Game of Life program we dimension an array V(512) to accommodate two 16 by 16 cell arrays.   Each cell array has 256 cells for a total of 512 in all. Since TBX arrays elements are numbered from 0, we could have gotten by with DIM V(511). A "1" in an array element represents a living cell; a "0" a dead cell. We avoid the use of a two-dimension arrays by applying the formula (16*row + column) to calculate the location of a desired cell. Also, rows 0 to 15 are Array 1 while row 15 to 31 are Array 2.

2. Multi-statement lines – The Game of Life program has several multi-statement lines. Lines 900 to 940 are good examples. Using multi-statement lines, we can collect together all cell initializations on a single array row.

```
900 I=5:J=7:V(16*I+J)=1
910 I=6:J=6:V(16*I+J)=1:J=7:V(16*I+J)=1:J=8:V(16*I+J)=1
920 I=7:J=6:V(16*I+J)=1:J=8:V(16*I+J)=1
930 I=8:J=6:V(16*I+J)=1:J=7:V(16*I+J)=1:J=8:V(16*I+J)=1
940 I=9:J=7:V(16*I+J)=1
```

Line 820 may require some explanation.

```
820 IF V(16*M+N)=0 THEN PRINT " ";:GOTO 830
```

If the relational expression is true, what part of the remainder of the line is executed? You may recall we elected to include all statements up to the CR byte.

Thus, both the PRINT and GOTO statements are executed only if the logical expression is true.

3. Logical Expressions – Consider now line 300 to 310.

300 IF V(16*M+N)=0 THEN IF A=3 THEN V(16*M+N)=1
305 IF V(16*M+N)=1 THEN IF A<2 THEN V(16*M+N)=0
310 IF V(16*M+N)=1 THEN IF A>3 THEN V(16*M+N)=0

Logically, each is a logical AND; i.e., both relational expressions must be true to execute the THEN statement. Using TBX's logical expression capability, we can replace the second IF statement with "&", the logical AND operator.

300 IF V(16*M+N)=0 & A=3 THEN V(16*M+N)=1
305 IF V(16*M+N)=1 & A<2 THEN V(16*M+N)=0
310 IF V(16*M+N)=1 & A>3 THEN V(16*M+N)=0

4. The RPT (Repeat) Statement – We see that line 120 is a simple one line loop.

120 GOSUB 200:J=J+1:IF J<=N+1 THEN GOTO 120

This fits nicely the form for the RPT statement, so we can speed things up by replacing it with

120 GOSUB 200:J=J+1:RPT J<=N+1

Look now at lines 110 to 130.

110 J=N-1
120 GOSUB 200:J=J+1:RPT J<=N+1
130 I=I+1:IF I<=M+1 THEN GOTO 110

We have a second loop that can be collapsed into the two lines with another RPT statement.

110 J=N-1
120 GOSUB 200:J=J+1:RPT J<=N+1:I=I+1:J=N-1:RPT I<=M+1

Line 130 was removed. A similar use of the RPT statement simplifies lines 705 to 715 changing from

```
705 C=0
710 V(16*I+C)=V(16*J+C):C=C+1:IF C<15 THEN GOTO 710
715 I=I+1:J=J+1:IF J<15 THEN GOTO 705
```

To

```
705 C=0
710 V(16*I+C)=V(16*J+C):C=C+1:RPT C<15:I=I+1:J=J+1:C=0:RPT j<15
```

More important than compressing the code, these changes speed up processing.

5. The READ Statement – In the original code, we use the LET statement in lines 900 to 940 to initialize the cells in the data array.

```
900 I=5:J=7:V(16*I+J)=1
910 I=6:J=6:V(16*I+J)=1:J=7:V(16*I+J)=1:J=8:V(16*I+J)=1
920 I=7:J=6:V(16*I+J)=1:J=8:V(16*I+J)=1
930 I=8:J=6:V(16*I+J)=1:J=7:V(16*I+J)=1:J=8:V(16*I+J)=1
940 I=9:J=7:V(16*I+J)=1
```

By replacing these lines with the READ statement, the living cell pattern can be visualized. See the highlighted characters.

```
900 I=5:J=7:READ    V(16*I+J)=1
910 I=6:J=6:READ V(16*I+J)=1,1,1
920 I=7:J=6:READ V(16*I+J)=1,0,1
930 I=8:J=6:READ V(16*I+J)=1,1,1
940 I=9:J=7:READ    V(16*I+J)=1
```

6. Preprocessing – By far the most spectacular improvement in speed comes with converting keywords to keyword codes before execution. Tests showed an amazing three fold speed increase. With the Game of Life running on the Cyclone V FPGA, the number of generations per minute jumped from 40 to over 120 with the Keyword Code modification!

Here is an image showing the first four generation of the Game of Life with these initial living cells.

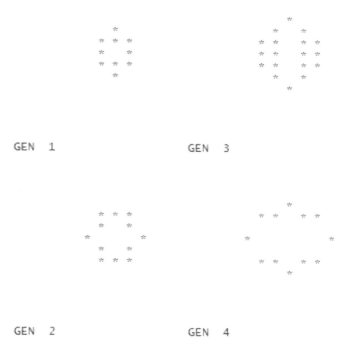

GEN 1

GEN 3

GEN 2

GEN 4

In the next chapter, we look at the Cyclone V FPGA implementation of the BYOC-24 CPU and how TBX performs.

Chapter 17
FPGA Implementation

While the Logisim simulation is suitable for development and experimentation, it's far too slow for any practical purpose. Nor can Logisim access external devices that might prove useful in developing real world applications. The Intel Cyclone V FPGA implementation described below provides just such a solution.

The Cyclone V GX Starter Kit is good choice for the beginner to experiment with a FPGA development platform. It includes an Intel Cyclone V GX (5CGXFC5C6F27C7N) FPGA and comes with an array of useful on-board hardware resources for experimentation. It is available from Mouser Electronics and Digikey Electronics.

To configure the GX Starter Kit board, we need Intel's Quartus IDE. Describing how to use Quartus is beyond the scope of this book. As with Logisim, the Internet offers numerous helpful video tutorials showing how to get started with Quartus. Quartus Prime Lite can be download free from http://fpgasoftware.intel.com/?edition=lite. Detailed instructions and software you need can be download via www.whippleway.com. Click on the "BYOC Resources" link in the left panel.

ZOC Terminal Emulator

We also need a PC terminal emulator. I highly recommend the ZOC Terminal The ZOC Terminal Emulator can be downloaded from https://www.emtec.com/zoc/terminal-emulator.html. Terminal emulators transmit PC keystrokes to the BYOC CPU via GX Starter Board's USB Data Port and displays information from the CPU on the PC. Follow these steps.

Step 1 – Connect a USB cable from your PC to the Cyclone V GX Starter board "UART to USB" port (the connector farthest from the 12 volt power socket.

Note: A quirk of the Cyclone V GX Starter Kit board is that the only one USB port can be connected at a time.   When configuring the ZOC Terminal Emulator, the USB Blaster port must not be connected.

Step 2 – Launch the ZOC Terminal Emulator, the starter page appears. Click "Quick Connection".

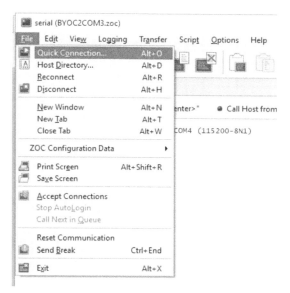

Step 3 – Select Serial Direct as the "Connection Type" and VT220 as the "Emulation". Then click "Edit..."

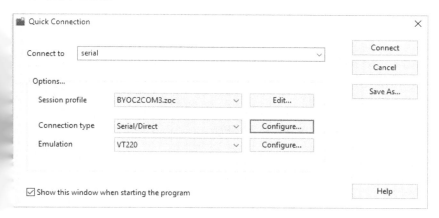

Step 3 – Click "Scan" to find and select the PC's communication port connected to the Cyclone V GX Starter board. Some experimentation may be needed here. Now select 155200 (serial data rate), 8N1 (8-bit data word with 1 stop bit), CD signal/pin is valid, and Break Signal 250 ms. Click "Save As" and give the Session Profile a name.

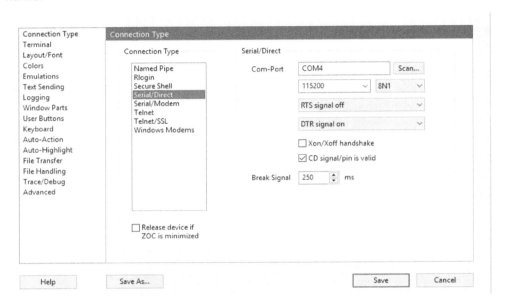

Step 4 – At this point, the Quick Connection screen reappears. The terminal emulator is ready to communicate with the BYOC CPU.

BYOC-24 CPU

Now move on to the next section to install the BYOC-24 CPU. One of the files you downloaded and unzipped is BYOC_24.sof. This is the Quartus file that configures the Cyclone V as the BYOC-24 CPU .

Follow the steps below to install the BYOC-24 CPU.

Step 1 – Connect a USB cable from your PC to the USB-Blaster Port (the one nearest the power connector) and power up the Cyclone V GX Starter board.

Note: A quirk of the Cyclone V GX Starter Kit board is that the only one USB port can be connected at a time.   When programming the board, the ZOC Terminal Emulator must not be connected.

Step 2 – Launch Quartus and click Tools-Programmer to launch the Programmer window.

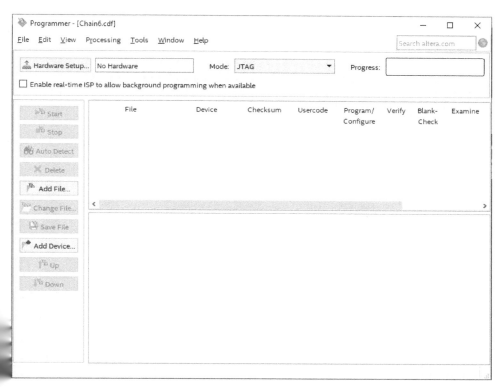

Step 3 – Click "Add File" and find the BYOC-24.sop file then click "Open".

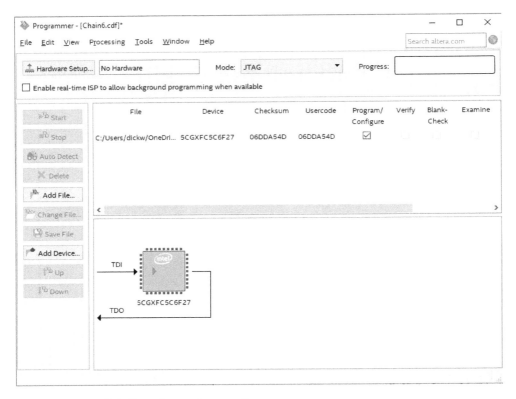

Step 4 – Next click "Hardware Setup…".

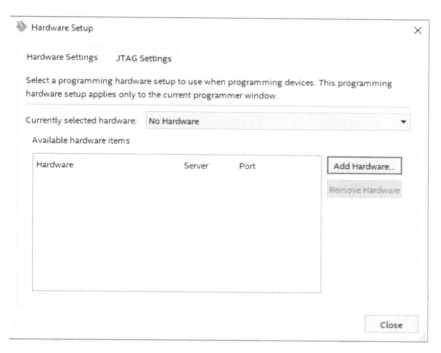

Hardware Setup   ×

Hardware Settings   JTAG Settings

Select a programming hardware setup to use when programming devices. This programming
hardware setup applies only to the current programmer window.

Currently selected hardware: No Hardware   ▼

Available hardware items

Hardware	Server	Port

Add Hardware...

Remove Hardware

Close

Step 5 – Click "Currently selected hardware" and choose the USB Blaster option.
click "Close".

Step 6 - In a few seconds, the Start button should turn active. Click on it and after a
short wait "Progress" should display "100%" indicating a successful download of the
BYOC-24 CPU.

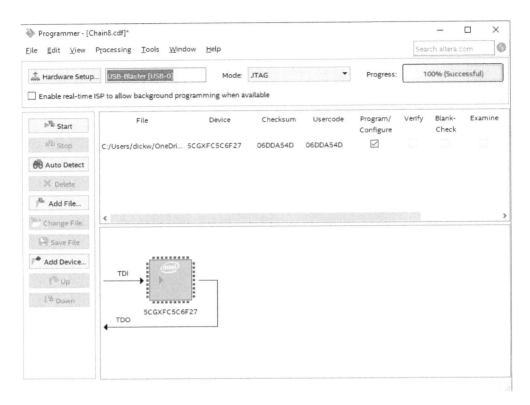

Step 7 - On the Cyclone V GX Starter board, switch SW0 should be in the up, the RUN position. Pressing button Key3 performs a hardware reset.

Step 8 – Switch the USB cables; that is, disconnect the programming cable and reconnect the ZOC Emulator cable. On the ZOC Emulator, click "File" then "Quick Connection" and "Connect".

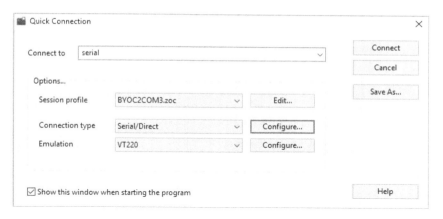

Step 9 – Press the KEY3 push button on the Cyclone V GX Starter board. Tiny BASIC Extended should be up and running with the sign-on message "Tiny BASIC Extended for the BYOC-24 CPU Version 1.0". See below.

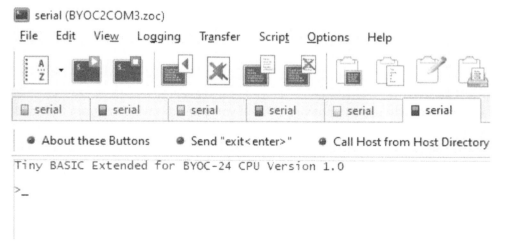

Preloaded TBX Programs

To try the preloaded programs, enter "load 0" then "run".

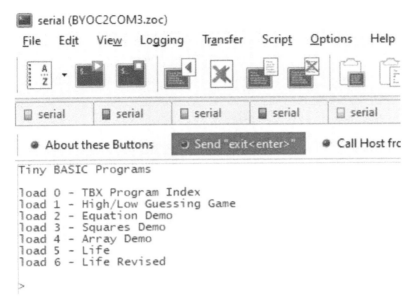

Enter "load " and the number to load the desired program. Enter "run" to execute it.

Save/Load Programs with ZOC

You are now ready to experiment with TBX. If you want to save a program and load it later, here's a way with the ZOC Terminal. List the program; select and copy it; then paste and save it as a simple text file.

```
>list

5 DIM V(512)
10 B=0:GOSUB 900:CLR
15 B=B+1:GOSUB 800
20 GOSUB 700
70 M=0
80 N=0
90 A=0
100 I=M-1
110 J=N-1
120 GOSUB 200:J=J+1:RPT J<=N+1:I=I+1:J=N-1:RPT I<=M+1
130 REM
140 GOSUB 300
150 N=N+1:IF N<=15 THEN GOTO 90
160 M=M+1:IF M<=15 THEN GOTO 80
170 GOTO 15
200 IF I=M THEN IF J=N THEN RETURN
205 K=I+16:L=J
210 IF K<16 THEN K=31
215 IF K>31 THEN K=16
220 IF J<0 THEN L=15
225 IF J>15 THEN L=0
230 A=A+V(16*K+L)
240 RETURN
300 IF V(16*M+N)=0 & A=3 THEN V(16*M+N)=1
305 IF V(16*M+N)=1 & A<2 THEN V(16*M+N)=0
310 IF V(16*M+N)=1 & A>3 THEN V(16*M+N)=0
315 RETURN
700 I=16:J=0
705 C=0
710 V(16*I+C)=V(16*J+C):C=C+1:RPT C<15:I=I+1:J=J+1:C=0:RPT j<15
715 REM
720 RETURN
800 CLR
810 M=0
815 N=0
820 IF V(16*M+N)=0 THEN PRINT " ";:GOTO 830
825 PRINT "*";
830 N=N+1:IF N<15 THEN GOTO 820
835 PRINT
840 M=M+1: IF M<15 THEN GOTO 815
845 PRINT "GEN ";B
850 RETURN
900 I=5:J=7:READ    V(16*I+J)=1
910 I=6:J=6:READ V(16*I+J)=1,1,1
920 I=7:J=6:READ V(16*I+J)=1,0,1
930 I=8:J=6:READ V(16*I+J)=1,1,1
940 I=9:J=7:READ    V(16*I+J)=1
950 RETURN
```

In this example, I save it using Notepad++ as "Life ZOC.txt".

To reload it, follow these steps:

Step 1 – In TBX, enter "new" to prepare for the new program.

Step 2- In ZOC Terminal, click on "Transfer" and then "Send Textfile …".

Step 3 - Select the program text file and click "Open"

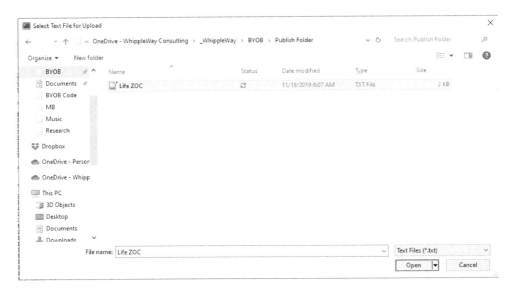

The ZOC Terminal sends the save program line-by-line to TBX. Don't be concerned that TBX prints a jumbled line of text as it receives the program lines. After the last line is sent, the program can be listed and run as if you keyed it in.

If you want experiment with TBX, I suggest you purchase and read my Amazon book "Build Your Own Computer – From Scratch". The assembly source code for TBX and a Python assembler are available from my website www.whippleway.com.

Chapter 18
Conclusion

I hope you have found the information in this book helpful in understanding how computer languages work. As I suggested at the outset, you should now be in a better position to understand and appreciate more fully what happens when they type "RUN", "COMPILE", or press the green "GO" button in whatever language you choose.

Whatever your future in computing may bring, I wish you the very best!

Comments and suggestions are welcome at byoc@whippleway.com.

Appendix A
BYOC-24 CPU Instruction Set

Abbreviations:

r_d, r_s	Register Code: 000 M 001 L 010 H 011 E 100 D 101 C 110 B 111 A
Z	Zero status bit
C	Carry status bit
V and v...v	8-bit constant value
V and v...v v...v	16-bit constant value
a and a...a	MS Byte 11111111 LS Byte aaaaaaaa (a ranges from 0 to 255)
A and a...a a...a	16-bit address
P and p...p	8-bit I/O port address
{..}	{Status Bits Affected}

MVI r_d,V	Move value to register	000 ddd 00 0000 0000 vvvvvvvv
MOV r_d,r_s	Move reg r_s to r_d	001 ddd sss 000 0000 00000000
MOV r_d,IRAML	Move index reg IRAM$_{0-7}$ to r_d	001ddd0000000 100 0000000
MOV r_d,IRAMH	Move index reg IRAM$_{8-15}$ to r_d	001ddd0000000 101 0000000
MOV r_d,IROML	Move index reg IROM$_{0-7}$ to r_d	001ddd0000000 110 0000000
MOV r_d,IROMH	Move index regr IROM$_{8-15}$ to r_d	001ddd0000000 111 0000000

LDR r_d,a	Load reg r_d direct Data RAM address 1..1a..a	010 ddd 000 0000 0 00 aaaaaaaa
STR a,r_s	Store reg r_s direct Data RAM address 1..1a..a	010 000 sss 0000 0 10 aaaaaaaa
LDX r_d,(IRAM)	Load reg r_d indirect Data RAM address in IRAM	010 ddd 000 0000 0 01 00000000
LDX r_d,(IROM)	Load reg r_d indirect Data ROM address in IROM	010 ddd 000 0000 0 11 00000000
STX (IRAM), r_s	Store reg r_s indirect Data RAM address in IRAM	010 000 sss 0000 1 10 00000000

LDHL IRAM	Load Data RAM index reg IRAM with HL	0110 0000 00000000 00000000
ADHL IRAM	Add HL to Data RAM index reg IRAM	0110 0001 00000000 00000000
CPHL IRAM	Compare Data RAM index reg IRAM to HL {C,Z}	0111 1001 00000000
INX IRAM	Increment Data RAM index reg IRAM	0110 0010 00000000 00000000
DCX IRAM	Decrement Data RAM index reg IRAM	0110 0011 00000000 00000000
LDHL IROM	Load Data ROM index reg IROM with HL	0110 0100 00000000 00000000
ADHL IROM	Add HL to Data ROM index reg IROM	0110 0100 00000000 00000000
CPHL IROM	Compare Data RAM index reg IROM to HL {C,Z}	0111 1101 00000000
INX IROM	Increment Data ROM index reg IROM	0110 0110 00000000 00000000
DCX IROM	Decrement Data ROM index reg IROM	0110 0111 00000000 00000000
LXI IRAM,V	Load Data RAM index reg IRAM immediate	0110 1000 vvvvvvvv vvvvvvvv

Mnemonic	Description	Encoding
LXI IROM,V	Load Data ROM index reg IROM immediate	0110 1100 vvvvvvvv vvvvvvvv
CPI IRAM,V	Compare Data RAM index reg IRAM immediate {C,Z}	0110 1001 vvvvvvvv vvvvvvvv
CPI IROM,V	Compare Data ROM index reg IROM immediate {C,Z}	0110 1101 vvvvvvvv vvvvvvvv
ADD r_d,r_s	Add regs: $r_d + r_s \rightarrow r_d$ & {C,Z}	100dddsss 0000 00000000000
SUB r_d,r_s	Subtract regs: $r_d - r_s \rightarrow r_d$ {C,Z}	100dddsss 0001 00000000000
ADC r_d,r_s	Add regs w/ carry: $r_d + r_s + c \rightarrow r_d$ {C,Z}	100dddsss 0010 00000000000
SBB r_d,r_s	Subtract regs w/ borrow: $r_d - r_s - b \rightarrow r_d$ {C,Z}	100dddsss 0011 00000000000
AND r_d,r_s	AND regs: r_d AND $r_s \rightarrow r_d$ {Z,C=0}	100dddsss 0100 00000000000
OR r_d,r_s	OR regs: r_d OR $r_s \rightarrow r_d$ {Z,C=0}	100dddsss 0101 00000000000
XOR r_d,r_s	XOR regs: r_d XOR $r_s \rightarrow r_d$ {Z,C=0}	100dddsss 0110 00000000000
NOT r_d,r_s	Invert reg: NOT $r_s \rightarrow r_d$ {Z,C=0}	100dddsss 0111 00000000000
ADI r_d,V	Add immediate to reg: $r_d + V \rightarrow r_d$ {C,Z}	100dddsss 0000 010 vvvvvvvv
SUI r_d,V	Subtr immediate from reg: $r_d - V \rightarrow r_d$ {C,Z}	100dddsss 0001 010 vvvvvvvv
ACI r_d,V	Add immediate to reg w/ carry: $r_d + V + c \rightarrow r_d$ {C,Z}	100dddsss 0010 010 vvvvvvvv
SBI r_d,V	Subtr immd from reg w/ borrow: $r_d - V - b \rightarrow r_d$ {C,Z}	100dddsss 0011 010 vvvvvvvv
ANI r_d,V	AND immediate reg r_d AND V $\rightarrow r_d$ {Z,C=0}	100dddsss 0100 010 vvvvvvvv
ORI r_d,V	OR immediate reg: r_d OR V $\rightarrow r_d$ {Z,C=0}	100dddsss 0101 010 vvvvvvvv
XRI r_d,V	XOR immediate reg: r_d XOR V $\rightarrow r_d$ {Z,C=0}	100dddsss 0110 010 vvvvvvvv
NTI r_d,V	Invert immediate: NOT V $\rightarrow r_d$ {Z,C=0}	100dddsss 0111 010 vvvvvvvv
RLC r_d	Rotate reg left: C <- 7..0 <- 0 {C}	100ddd000 1000 000 00000000
RRC r_d	Rotate reg right: 0 -> 7..0 -> C {C}	100ddd000 1001 000 00000000
RAL r_d	Rotate reg left through carry: C <- 7..0 <- 0 {C}	100ddd000 1010 000 00000000
RAR r_d	Rotate reg right through carry: C -> 7..0 -> {C}	100ddd000 1011 000 00000000
INR r_d	Increment reg r_d: $r_d + 1 \rightarrow r_d$ {Z }	100ddd000 1100 000 00000000
DCR r_d	Decrement reg r_d: $r_d - 1 \rightarrow r_d$ {Z}	100ddd000 1101 000 00000000
STC	Set carry {C}	100ddd000 1110 000 00000000
CMP r_d,r_s	Subtract regs: $r_d - r_s$; $r_d \rightarrow r_d$ {Z,C}	100dddsss0001 001 000000000
CPI r_d,V	Subtr immediate from reg: $r_d - V$; $\rightarrow r_d$ {Z,C}	100dddsss0001 011 vvvvvvvv
INP r_d,P	Input from I/O port P to reg r_d: I/O Port p $\rightarrow r_d$	01 ddd 000 0000 000 pppppppp
OUT P,r_s	Output to I/O port P from reg r_s: I/O Port p $\rightarrow r_s$	101 000 sss 0000 001 pppppppp
POP r_d	Pop top of PP Stack to reg r_d	101 ddd 000 0000 010 00000000
PUSH r_s	Push reg r_s on top of PP Stack	101 000 sss 0000 011 00000000
CALL A aaaaaaaa	Call subroutine at address A	11000000 aaaaaaaa
RET 0000000000000000	Return from subroutine	11010000
RZ 0000000000000000	Return from subroutine on zero	11011000
RNZ 0000000000000000	Return from subroutine on not zero	11011100
RC	Return from subroutine on carry	11011010 0000000000000000

145

RNC	Return from subroutine on not carry	11011110 0000000000000000
JZ A	Jump on zero to address a...a	11100000 aaaaaaaa aaaaaaaa
JNZ A	Jump on not zero to address a...a	11100100 aaaaaaaa aaaaaaaa
JC A	Jump on carry to address a...a	11101000 aaaaaaaa aaaaaaaa
JNC A	Jump on not carry to address a...a	11101100 aaaaaaaa aaaaaaaa
JMP A	Jump to address a...a	11110000 aaaaaaaa aaaaaaaa
PCHL	Jump to address in HL	11110010 00000000 00000000

Appendix B
High/Low Guessing Game

The following is the BYOC-24 assembly language code for the High/Low Guessing Game.

```
 1   Label    Operation      Operand  Comment
 2   ;
 3   ;   High/Low Guessing Game for Logisim BYOC-24
 4   ;
 5   ;  Copyright 2019 by Dick Whipple
 6   ;
 7   ;   Set-Up Code
 8   ;
 9   setup:  call     clr_scr ;Clear screen
10           lxi      irom,msg0        ;Display title message
11           call     mout
12   ;
13   ;  Main Routine
14   ;
15   main:   call     new_line         ;Skip line
16           call     new_line
17           lxi      irom,msg1        ;Display instructions
18           call     mout
19           call     new_line         ;Next line
20           lxi      irom,msg2        ;Continue print instructions
21           call     mout
22           call     get_rnd_num      ;Get random number to guess
23           str      unknown,e        ;Store unknown random value
24           mvi      e,0              ;Zero tries counter D
25           str      tries,e
26   get_guess:      call     new_line;Next line
27           lxi      irom,msg3        ;Print guess request
28           call     mout
29           call     buf_in           ;Get guess into buffer
30           ldr      e,tries          ;Incement counter
31           adi      e,1
32           str      tries,e
33           call     dinp             ;Get guess into C from buffer
34           ldr      a,unknown        ;Get unknown into A
35           cmp      d,a              ;Compare guess in C to unknown in A?
36           jz       got_it           ;If equal, branch to Got It
37           jnc      high             ;If guess C greater than E, branch to high
38   low:    lxi      irom,msg7        ;If less, display "Too Low" message
39   finish: call     mout
40           jmp      get_guess        ;Do again
41   high:   lxi      irom,msg6        ;Display "Too High" message and do again
42           jmp      finish
43   got_it: lxi      irom,msg4        ;Display "Got It" message and number tries
44           call     mout
45           ldr      d,tries          ;Get number of tries into D
46           call     dout             ;Display number of tries
47           lxi      irom,msg5
48           call     mout
49           jmp      main             ;Do over from main entry point
```

```
50   ;
51   ;  Buffer Input Routine
52   ;
53   buf_in: mvi      h,hi(buf_start) ;Point HL to start of buffer
54        mvi      l,lo(buf_start)
55        mvi      e,0             ;Zero input buffer count
56        str      buf_count,e
57   buf_in_0:        call    din      ;Get a charater in D and print it
58        cpi      d,bs    ;Is it a back space?
59        jnz      buf_in_2        ;If not, continue…
60        ldr      e,buf_count     ;At buffer start?
61        or       e,e
62        jz       buf_in_0        ;If so, do nothing and get next character
63        sui      e,1             ;Otherwise, counter back one character
64        str      buf_count,e
65   buf_in_1:        sui      a,1      ;Buffer address back one character
66        jmp      buf_in_0        ;Get next character
67   buf_in_2:        mov      m,d      ;Save at HL
68        ldr      e,buf_count     ;Advance buffer count by 1
69        adi      e,1
70        str      buf_count,e
71        inr      l               ;Advance buffer address one character
72        jnz      buf_in_3
73        inr      h
74   buf_in_3:        cpi      d,eol    ;Check for end ofline character
75        jnz      buf_in_0        ;If not, do again
76        ret                      ;Otherwise, done and return
77   ;
78   ;  Input Single Character to B from Keyboard
79   ;
80   din:    inp      d,cntr_port    ;Get keyboard character into A
81        ani      d,0b01000000   ;Character available?
82        jz       din            ;If not, keep checking
83        inp      d,data_port    ;Get the ASCII character
84        mov      e,d
85        jmp      eout           ;Display it
86   ;
87   ; Get Random Number 0 to 100 in E
88   ;
89   get_rnd_num:     call    new_line;New line
90        lxi      irom,msg8      ;Display 'Press any key…" message
91        call     mout           ;Print message
92   get_rnd_num_0:   inp a,cntr_port ;Get keyboard control byte
93        ani      a,64           ;Is character available?
94        jz       get_rnd_num_0  ;If not, keep checking
95        inp      a,data_port    ;If so, clear keyboard data port
96        inp      e,rnd_port     ;Get a random number
97   get_rnd_num_1:   sui      e,101    ;Compute modulo 100
98        jnc      get_rnd_num_1
99        adi      e,101
100       ret                      ;Return to calling routine
```

```
100         ret                     ;Return to calling routine
101     ;
102     ;   Convert ASCII number at BUF_START to binary in D
103     ;
104  dinp:   mvi     d,0             ;Preset D for single digit result
105          mvi     h,hi(buf_start) ;Point HL to start of buffer
106          mvi     l,lo(buf_start)
107          mov     e,m             ;Get ASCII character
108          cpi     e,eol           ;Is it the end-of-line?
109          rz                      ;If so, done and exit.
110  dinp_0: sui     e,48            ;If not, remove ASCII bias
111          add     d,e             ;Add to preset value
112          inr     l               ;Point HL to next character
113          jnz     dinp_l
114          inr     h
115  dinp_l: cpi     m,eol           ;If so, done and exit
116          mov     e,d             ;Multiply exisitng value by 10
117          add     d,d
118          add     d,d
119          add     d,e
120          add     d,d
121          mov     e,m             ;Get next character
122          jmp     dinp_0          ;Do again
123     ;
124     ;   Convert Number in D to ASCII and Display It
125     ;
126     ;     zero_supr is a flag used to suppress output of leading zeros except when D is zero
127     ;
128  dout:   mvi     a,0             ;Zero zero-suppression flag
129          str     zero_supr,a
130          mvi     e,100           ;Check and display 100's digit
131          call    cnvrt
132          mvi     e,10            ;Check and display 10's digit
133          call    cnvrt
134          mov     e,d             ;Display remainder in D as 1's digit
135          adi     e,48            ;Add ASCII bias
136          call    eout            ;Display it
137          ret                     ;Done
138     ;
139     ;   Print Positional Digit in DE
140     ;
141  cnvrt:  mvi     a,255           ;Set zero suppress flag to -1
142  cnvrt_0:        adi a,l         ;Increment it
143          sub     d,e             ;Subtract digit value E from D
144          jnc     cnvrt_0         ;If result positive, subtract again
145          add     d,e             ;If negative, add digit value back to D
146          ldr     e,zero_supr     ;Get zero suppress flag into E
147          cmp     a,e             ;Does result match zero suppress flag?
148          jnz     cnvrt_l         ;If not, print it
149          ret                     ;Otherwise, done
150  cnvrt_l:sui     e,l             ;Turn off zero suppression
151          str     zero_supr,e
152          mov     e,a             ;Get digit to display into E
153          adi     e,48            ;Add ASCII bias
154          jmp     eout            ;Display it
```

```
155  ;
156  ;  Display Single Character in E Register
157  ;
158  eout:    str      eout_temp,e    ;Save E
159  eout_0: inp      e,cntr_port    ;Is TTY busy
160           ani      e,128
161           jnz      eout_0         ;If so, wait
162           ldr      e,eout_temp    ;Restore E
163           out      data_port,e    ;IDisplay character
164           ret                     ;Done
165  ;
166  ;  Display New Line
167  ;
168  new_line: mvi    e,eol           ;Load E with new line character
169            jmp    eout            ;Display it
170  ;
171  ;  Clear Screen
172  ;
173  clr_scr: mvi    e,cntr_l         ;Load E with clear screen character
174           jmp    eout            ;Display it
175  ;
176  ;  Display Message at address A in Data ROM
177  ;
178  ;    Message terminates with 0x00 byte
179  ;
180  mout:    ldx      e,irom         ;Get character from Data ROM
181           or       e,e            ;Is it zero?
182           rz                      ;If so, done
183           call     eout           ;If not, display it
184           inx      irom           ;Point to next character
185           jmp      mout           ;Do again
186  ;
187  ;  End Program - Begin Data Section
188  ;
189  data
190  msg0:    Number Guessing Game
191  msg1:    I am thinking of a number
192  msg2:    between 1 and 100.
193  msg3:    Your guess?
194  msg4:    You got it in
195  msg5:     tries.
196  msg6:    Too high.  Try again.
197  msg7:    Too low.  Try again.
198  msg8:    Press any key to continue...
```

```
199   cr       equ     13      ;Carriage return character
200   lf       equ     10      ;Line feed character
201   eol      equ     10      ;End-of-line character
202   cntr_l   equ     12      ;Clear screen character
203   bs       equ     8       ;Back space character
204   buf_start        equ     0         ;Start of character buffer
205   cntr_port        equ     0         ;Terminal Unit control port
206   data_port        equ     1         ;Terminal Unit data port
207   rnd_port         equ     2         ;Randon Unit data port
208   unknown equ      0       ;Unknown value to be guessed
209   tries    equ     1       ;Number of tries
210   buf_count        equ     2         ;Input buffer counter
211   zero_supr        equ     3         ;Zero supression flag
212   eout_temp        equ     4         ;EOUT temporary value
213   ;
214   ;  End Data Section
215   ;
216   end
```

Appendix C
Data RAM Storage

The first three variables (bufstrt, varStart, and prgmem) are located beginning at Data RAM 0. The remaining variable are stored in the last 256 bytes of the Data RAM. The listing below shows addresses calculated relative to 0xFF00.

```
;
;  Data RAM Map
;
ram_start    equ    0              ;Start of Data RAM
;
bufstrt      equ    ram_start      ;Keyboard input buffer
;
varstrt      equ    bufstrt+72     ;Space for 26 16-bit (two byte) variables A-Z
;
prgmem       equ    varstrt+52     ;Start of Tiny BASIC program space
;
curlbl       equ    0              ;Current line number
prgstrt      equ    curlbl+2       ;First byte of Tiny BASIC program
prgend       equ    prgstrt+2      ;Last byte of Tiny BASIC program + 1
txtstrt      equ    prgend+2       ;Start of text for curent line
count        equ    txtstrt+2      ;Length of text in keybord input buffer
case         equ    count+1        ;Reserve for future use
zone         equ    case+1         ;Zone counter
aelvl        equ    zone+1         ;Reserve for future use
indx         equ    aelvl+2        ;Reserve for future use
sbrlvl       equ    indx+1         ;Reserve for future use
astrt        equ    sbrlvl+2       ;Reserve for future use
seed1        equ    astrt+2        ;RANDOM NUMBER SEED 1
seed2        equ    seed1+1        ;RANDOM NUMBER SEED 2
seed3        equ    seed2+1        ;RANDOM NUMBER SEED 3
seed4        equ    seed3+1        ;RANDOM NUMBER SEED 4
mend         equ    seed4+1        ;End of program memory
```

Appendix D
Tiny BASIC Subroutine Library

Listed below are the subroutine used in the BYOC-24 CPU version of Tiny BASIC. The format for each description is as follows:

Subroutine Name – {In: Called Parameters} {Out: Return Values} Description

Because of the complexities of many of these subroutines, <u>assume that all registers are used</u>. The only exceptions are the index registers IRAM and IROM.

add – {In: Top two Tiny BASIC values on top of PP Stack} {Out: Sum of top two Tiny BASIC values on the PP Stack } Adds the top two values on the PP Stack.

asc2bin – {In: Program byte address in IRAM} {Out: Register A contains the numeric value of an ASCII number character} Checks if register A contains a numeric ASCII character (0 to 9). If so, returns with the numeric value and the carry status set. If not, returns with carry status reset.

chknum – {In: Register A contains a character byte} {Out: None} Checks if register A contains a numeric ASCII character (0 to 9). If so, returns with carry status set. If not, returns with carry status reset.

ckpend – {In: Value in register pair HL} {Out: None} Checks if HL (representing an address) is equal to the program end address "prgend". If so, returns with zero status set. If not, returns with zero status reset.

chrin – {In: None} {Out: A contains character inputted from keyboard} Inputs an ASCII character from the keyboard.

chrout – {In: Register A contains the character to be printed} {Out: None} Prints the ASCII character in the A register.

cinit: – {In: None} {Out: None} Initializes the program section of Data RAM for entering a new Tiny BASIC program.

crlf – {In: None} {Out: None} Skips to next line.

clrscr – {In: None} {Out: None} Clears the display.

cnvrt – {In: Register pair HL contains value to be printed; register pair DE contains the positional value (1, 10, 100, …) of the target digit to be converted; register C contains zero-suppression flag} {Out: None} Works in conjunction with the "numout" subroutine converting to ASCII and printing the value of the target digit. If register C is zero when call, leading zeros are not printed. If not zero, leading zeros are printed.

div – {In: Top two Tiny BASIC values on top of PP Stack} {Out: Quotient of top two Tiny BASIC values on the PP Stack } Divides the top two values on the PP Stack. The second is divided by the first.

expr – {In: Program byte address in IRAM} {Out: Tiny BASIC expression value on top of PP Stack} Evaluates the Tiny BASIC expression at IRAM returning with the expression's value on top of the PP Stack. Upon return, IRAM points passed the expression.

factor – {In: Program byte address in IRAM} {Out: Tiny BASIC expression factor value on top of PP Stack} Evaluates the Tiny BASIC expression factor at IRAM returning with the factor's value on top of the PP Stack. Upon return, IRAM points passed the factor.

fndlbl – {In: Register pair DE contains the line number to be found} {Out: Register pair HL contains the starting address of the found line} Searches the program for the line number in DE. If found, returns with starting address of line and the carry status set. If not found, returns with carry status reset.

getfnct – {In: Program byte address in IRAM} {Out: Function value on top of PP Stack} Checks if a function keyword is present in a Tiny BASIC expression. If so, executes the associated function code leaving the function value on top of the PP Stack. Returns with the carry status set and IRAM pointing passed the function keyword. If no function is found, returns with carry status reset.

getkey – {In: Program byte address in IRAM} {Out: Register C contains the numeric position (base 0) of found keyword in keyword table} Searches the keyword table for the possible keyword starting at the address in IRAM. If found, the carry is set for the return and IRAM points passed the keyword. If not found, the carry is reset for the return and IRAM is unchanged.

getline – {In: None} {Out: None} Copies keyboard input to Data RAM's input buffer starting at "bufstrt". Terminates with a carriage return CR keystroke. Erases the previous byte with a back space BS keystroke.

getlink – {In: Register C contains the numeric position (base 0) of a keyword in keyword table } {Out: Register pair HL contains the address of the routine to process the keyword} Uses the C register value to calculate the address in the in the keyword link table of the routine that processes the associated keyword.

getnum – {In: Program byte address in IRAM} {Out: Constant value on top of PP Stack} Checks if a constant is present in a Tiny BASIC expression. If so, it puts the constant's value on top of the PP Stack. Returns with the carry status set and IRAM pointing passed the constant. If no constant is found, returns with carry status reset.

getvar – {In: Program byte address in IRAM} {Out: Variable value on top of PP Stack} Checks if a variable is present in a Tiny BASIC expression. If so, it puts the variable's value on top of the PP Stack. Returns with the carry status set and IRAM pointing passed the variable. If no variable is found, returns with carry status reset.

getvaradrs – {In: Program byte address in IRAM} {Out: If variable found, register pair HL contains the variables address} Checks for the presence of a variable. If found, returns with the address of the variable in HL, the carry status set, and IRAM pointing passed variable. If no variable found, returns with carry status reset and IRAM unchanged.

insrt – {In: None} {Out: None} Given that a new program line is in the input buffer, the following operations are performed: (1) If the line has text and the line number does not exist, the new line is inserted. (2) If the line has text and the line number exists, the current line is deleted before the new line is inserted. (3) If the line has no text and the line number exists in the program, the current line is deleted.

memtest – {In: Value in register pair HL} {Out: None} Checks if HL (representing an address) is greater than the program end address "prgend". If so, returns with carry set. If not, returns with carry reset.

msgout – {In: Message address in IROM } {Out: None} Prints message (ASCII character string) pointed to by address in IROM. Zero byte (0x00) terminates message.

modulo – {In: Top two Tiny BASIC values on top of PP Stack} {Out: Modulo of top two Tiny BASIC values on the PP Stack } Divides the top two values on the PP Stack placing the remainder on top of the PP Stack. The second is divided by the first.

mul – {In: Top two Tiny BASIC values on top of PP Stack} {Out: Product of top two Tiny BASIC values on the PP Stack } Multiplies the top two values on the PP Stack.

ninox – {In: Register pair HL contains 16-bit value; B register contains the number negative values encountered in a multiplication or division} {Out: Register pair HL contains twos-complement of original value; B register incremented} Performs twos-complement operation on value in HL and increments the B register.

neg – {In: Tiny BASIC value on top of PP Stack} {Out: Negated Tiny BASIC value on top of PP Stack} Negates the value on top of the PP Stack.

numout – {In: Register pair HL contains value to be printed; register C contains zero-suppression flag} {Out: None} Converts to ASCII and prints the 16-bit value in register pair HL. If register C is zero when call, leading zeros are not printed. If not zero, leading zeros are printed.

printlit – {In: Program byte address in IRAM} {Out: None} If an opening quotation mark is found at the IRAM address, the following ASCII characters up to the closing quote are printed. Upon return, IRAM points passed the closing quotation mark.

printnum – {In: Value to be printed on top of P Stack} {Out: None} Converts to ASCII and prints the 16-bit, twos-complement value on top of the PP Stack.

skipspace – {In: Program byte address in IRAM} {Out: IRAM points to first non-space character; Register A contains the first non-space character} Increments IRAM as necessary to skip ASCII spaces in the program line.

store– {In: Value to be stored on top of PP Stack; Target variable address next on PP Stack} {Out: None} Stores value on top of PP Stack at the address of the variable next on the PP Stack.

sub – {In: Top two Tiny BASIC values on top of PP Stack} {Out: Difference of top two Tiny BASIC values on the PP Stack } Subtracts the top two values on the PP Stack. The second is subtracted from the first.

term – {In: Program byte address in IRAM} {Out: Tiny BASIC expression term value on top of PP Stack} Evaluates the Tiny BASIC expression term at IRAM returning with the term's value on top of the PP Stack. Upon return, IRAM points passed the term.

trns – {In: None} {Out: None} Translates keywords to keyword codes within the input buffer.

tstl – {In: None} {Out: None} If, after skipping any spaces, a line number is found in the Data RAM's input buffer, it is converted to 16-bit binary and stored in "curlbl". Upon returning, the carry status is set (made "1") and IRAM points to the first byte passed the line number. If no line number is found, zero (0x0000) is stored in "curlbl". Upon returning, the carry status is reset (made "0") and IRAM points to the first non-space character.

twocmp – {In: Register pair HL contains 16-bit value} {Out: Register pair HL contains twos-complement of original value} Performs twos-complement operation on value in HL.

winit– {In: None} {Out: None} Performs any functions to terminate executing program in preparation for a return to Editor/Command Mode.

xhlde – {In: Register pair HL contains a value; register pair DE contains a value} {Out: HL contains DE's original value; DE contains HL's original value} Exchanges the contents of register pairs HL and DE.

Appendix E
Random Number Generator

Tiny BASIC's random number routine uses a variation of the *linear congruential generator* method to generate a sequence of random numbers. Four bytes in Data RAM ("seed1…seed4) are manipulated in a way that generates a series of pseudo-random, 16-bit numbers. In turn, these are reduced to the range of 0 to 1000 and used by the RND function. For more information on the method itself, see https://en.wikipedia.org/wiki/Linear_congruential_generator.

```
 1   ;
 2   ;        RNDM - PUTS RANDOM NTEGER (0-1000)ON AE STACK
 3   ;
 4   ; Shift-register pseudorandom number generator
 5   ; Calculating successive powers of seed4..seed1
 6   ;
 7   rndm:   call    skipspace     ;Get next nonspace character
 8           cpi     a,'('         ;Should be an open parentheses?
 9           jnz     err0          ;If not, raise syntax error
10           inx     iram          ;Point next character
11           call    expr          ;Get option parameter
12           call    skipspace     ;Get next nonspace character
13           cpi     a,')'         ;Should be a closed parentheses
14           jnz     err0          ;If not, raise syntax error
15           inx     iram
16           pop     l
17           pop     h
18           cpi     1,0           ;Is it 0 - new random number?
19           jz      rndml0        ;If so, continue here
20           cpi     1,1           ;Is it 1 - randomize first
21           jz      rndmz         ;If so, continue here
22           cpi     1,2           ;Is it 2 - restart the random sequence first
23           jz      rndmrst       ;If so, continue here
24           jmp     err12         ;Invalid function parameter error
25   rndml0: mvi     h,0xff        ;Start randomizing manipulation
26           mvi     l,seed4
27           mvi     b,8
28   rndml1: mov     a,m
29           rlc     a
30           aci     a,0
31           rlc     a
32           aci     a,0
33           rlc     a
34           aci     a,0
35           xor     a,m
36           ral     a
37           ral     a
38           dcr     l
39           dcr     l
40           dcr     l
41           mov     a,m
42           ral     a
43           mov     m,a
44           inr     l
45           mov     a,m
46           ral     a
47           mov     m,a
48           inr     l
49           mov     a,m
50           ral     a
```

```
51          mov     m,a
52          inr     l
53          mov     a,m
54          ral     a
55          mov     m,a
56          dcr     b
57          jnz     rndml1
58          ldr     h,seed3
59          ldr     l,seed4
60          ani     h,0x03          ;Keep to less than 1000
61          cpi     h,0x03
62          jz      rndmc2
63  rndmc1: jnc     rndml0
64          push    h
65          push    l
66          stc                     ;Set carry and return
67          ret
68  rndmc2: cpi     l,0xe8
69          jmp     rndmc1
70  ;
71  getfncte:stc                    ;Set carry and return
72          ret
73  ;
74  ; Randomize Seed
75  ;
76  rndmz:  inp     a,2             ;Do random access to counter port
77          str     seed1,a
78          ani     a,0x7
79  rndmz1: dcr     a               ;Do it random multiple of times
80          jnz     rndmz1
81          inp     a,2             ;One last time
82          ral     a               ;Manipulate it
83          xri     a,0b10101010
84          str     seed2,a
85          jmp     rndml0          ;Get the randomized number
86  ;
87  ; Reset to Starting Random Seeds
88  ;
89  rndmrst:lxi     irom,seed_data  ;Get original seeds
90          ldx     a,(irom)        ;Store them
91          str     seed1,a
92          inx     irom
93          ldx     a,(irom)
94          str     seed2,a
95          inx     irom
96          ldx     a,(irom)
97          str     seed3,a
98          inx     irom
99          ldx     a,(irom)
100         str     seed4,a
101         jmp     rndml0          ;Get random number
```

Appendix F
Logisim Debugger

The Logisim version of the BYOC-24 CPU has a very elementary debugger. See the figure below.

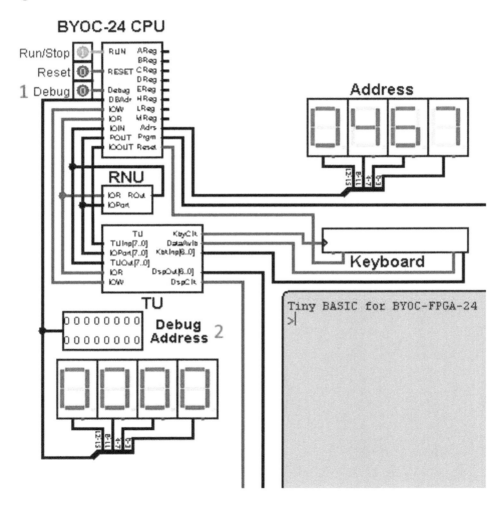

1. When the debug control input is "0", the debugger is disabled. When it is "1", the debugger is enabled.

2. When Debug is "1" and the executing address is the same as the Debug Address, the BYOC-24 CPU enters a halt state. Returning Debug to "0", execution continues.

The following example demonstrates how the debugger can be used:

Step 1 – Determine from the assembly listing where you want execution to halt. This address is called a *breakpoint*. See below.

STMPRC:	MOV A,IRAML	001B	3C0200
	STR TXTSTRT,A	001C	438206
	MOV A,IRAMH	001D	3C0280
	STR TXTSTRT+1,A	001E	438207
	CALL SKIPSPACE	001F	C00175
	CALL GETKEY	0020	C0017A
→	JNC LET	0021	EC0037
STMPRC0:	CALL GETLINK	0022	C001A1
	PCHL	0023	F20000
DONE:	CALL SKIPSPACE	0024	C00175
DONEC0:	CPI A,CR	0025	9C0B0D

In this example, we want to inspect the value of the C register after calling "getkey", so the breakpoint is 0x0021.

Step 2 – Set the Debug Address to 0x0021 and Debug to "1".

Step 3 – Enter and run the sample program. We are looking for the value of C when executing a PRINT statement. Here is the result.

(Next page please)

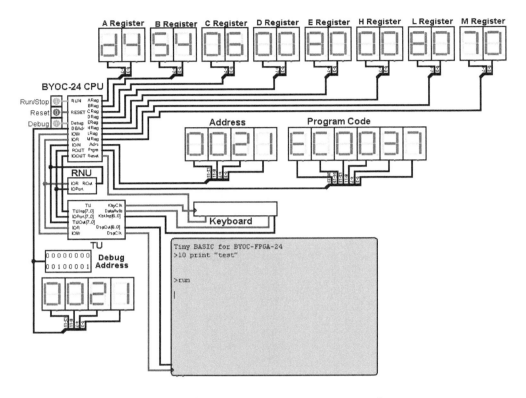

Execution halts at 0x0021 and register C is 6 as was expected.

Step 4 – At this point, we have a couple of options.

    (a) Set another breakpoint.
        1. Press control K to stop the clock.
        2. Change the Debug Address to the new breakpoint.
        3. Press control K again to start the clock.
        4. Execution continues to the next breakpoint.
    (b) Single step through the code
        1. Press control K to stop the clock.
        2. Change Debug to "0".
        3. Press control T multiple times to step through the code.

While debugging, you can view the BYOC-24 CPU by right clicking and selecting "View BYOC-24". This can be very useful when using option (b).

Appendix G
Tiny BASIC Development Cycle

If you are not familiar with program development with Tiny BASIC, here is a brief synopsis.

1. Outline the logical flow of the program in a functional flowchart. Consider which Tiny BASIC statements and variables will implement each process block. Identify any process blocks that lend themselves to becoming subroutines. Ensure that there are no overlapping loops.

2. Enter the NEW command. This removes any previous program from memory and resets all program specific parameters.

3. Enter the program line-by-line.

4. Enter the LIST command to print and check your program.

5. Enter the "RUN" command to execute the program.

6. To exit the program, either include a "STOP" statement at the appropriate point or press the "Esc" (Escape) key.

7. Optionally add the program to the assembled version of Tiny BASIC so that you can use the LOAD command to load and run it later.

[i] Historically, so called "batch" programs on main frame computers utilized this flow pattern.

[ii] RAM Random Access Memory is a form of computer memory that can be read and changed in any order, typically used to store working data and machine code. It's usually volatile, meaning it is lost when power is interrupted. https://en.wikipedia.org/wiki/Random-access_memory

[iii] ROM Read Only Memory is a type of non-volatile memory used in computers and other electronic devices. Data stored in ROM cannot be electronically modified after the manufacture of the memory device. Read-only memory is useful for storing software that is rarely changed during the life of the system, sometimes known as firmware. https://en.wikipedia.org/wiki/Read-only_memory

[iv] ASCII abbreviated from American Standard Code for Information Interchange, is a character encoding standard for electronic communication. ASCII codes represent text in computers, telecommunications equipment, and other devices. Most modern character-encoding schemes are based on ASCII, although they support many additional characters.

[v] The push/pop stack is used "PUSH r" and "POP r" BYOB-24 CPU instructions to save and restore registers. The call/return stack is used with BYOC-24 "CALL a" and "RET" instructions to access machine language subroutines.

Printed in France by Amazon
Brétigny-sur-Orge, FR

14572062R00099